JEANETTE
Unleash your
inner Rain

# RAINMAKER:

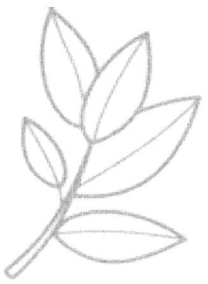

# UNLEASHED

by
Sejal Bhasker Patel

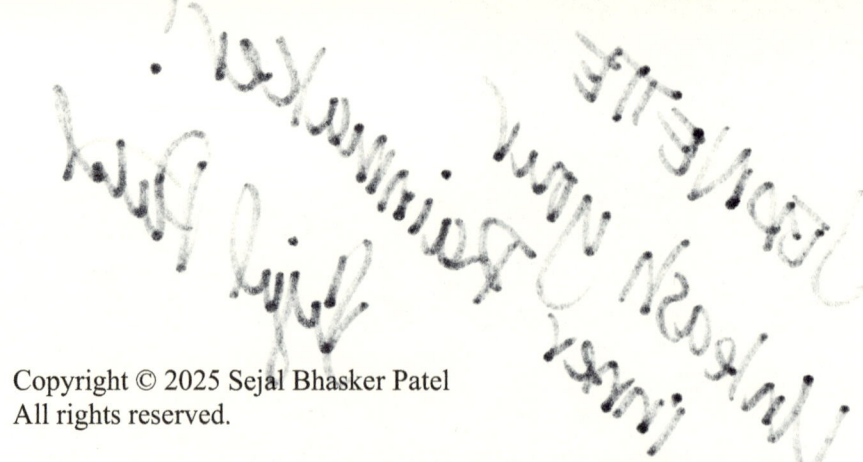

Copyright © 2025 Sejal Bhasker Patel
All rights reserved.

No part of this publication may be reproduced, distributed, or transmitted in any form or by any means—including photocopying, recording, or other electronic or mechanical methods—without the prior written permission of the copyright owner, except in the case of brief quotations used in reviews, articles, or academic works, with proper attribution.

This book is a work of original nonfiction based on the author's personal experiences and professional expertise. While specific stories are true to the best of the author's knowledge, identifying details have been changed to protect individual privacy. The strategies and opinions presented are for informational purposes only and are not intended as legal or business advice.

For licensing inquiries, firm-wide distribution, or rainmaking consulting, please contact:
Sage Ivy Consulting
www.sageivyconsulting.com

Rainmaker: Unleashed
ISBN: 978-1-968594-00-8
Cover design by AMZ Pro Publisher
Published by Sage Ivy Consulting
New York, NY

Printed in the United States of America
First edition

# Dedication:

To my dad—
Who came to this country on a student visa, led by brilliance and grit.
Thank you for law school.
Thank you for the wisdom that shaped me.
You've been the rock of my life—and the light in every dark season.

And to Aiden—
My favorite nephew. The future of this family.
Your smart-ass wit, wild spirit, and bright mind give me so much hope.
You make this world lighter just by being in it.

"The journey of a thousand miles begins with a single step."

—Lao Tzu

# Table of Contents

Author's Note

Introduction: The Book I Wish Existed

Chapter 1: Made Partner? Now Bring in Business. ............................................. xiii

Chapter 2: Not All Rainmakers Look Alike ........................................................ 9

Chapter 3: Your Network Isn't Flat—It's Untapped ........................................... 15

Chapter 4: Conversations Aren't One-Night Stands .......................................... 24

Chapter 5: Pack Strategy, Not Just Business Cards ........................................... 30

Chapter 6: Walk In With a Plan, Not a Panic Attack ......................................... 36

Chapter 7: Small Talk Doesn't Mean Small Impact .......................................... 41

Chapter 8: Don't be a Wallflower ...................................................................... 49

Chapter 9: The Hidden Cost of Being 'On.' ....................................................... 54

Chapter 10: Still Thinking About That Great Conversation? They're Not. ........ 61

Chapter 11: CLEs Done Right = Clients in the Room ...................................... 66

Chapter 12: Visibility Without Strategy Is Just Noise ...................................... 72

Chapter 13: Rainmaking Isn't Earned—It's Claimed ........................................ 78

Chapter 14: Not Everyone Needs to Be a Client ............................................... 88

Chapter 15: Apparently I Missed the Memo on Golf and Scotch ...................... 95

Chapter 16: So Busy. When Do I Do This? ..................................................... 101

Chapter 17: How Freedom Is Built ................................................................... 110

Chapter 18: Associates – Your Secret Sauce .................................................... 119

Chapter 19: It's Not Confidence. It's Knowing My Value. ............................... 126

Chapter 20: The Inside Scoop (*formerly known as The Mysterious Client*) ..... 134

Chapter 21: Origination = Power ...................................................................... 143

Epilogue: This Was Always About Power ....................................................... 154

About the Author .............................................................................................. 155

Rainmaker: Unleashed

## *Author's Note:*

*You think I have extra time to write a book? While I'm launching a company, writing columns for Above the Law, leading workshops, and advising clients?*

**No.**
**I wrote this book because I had to.**

*I was sick of watching brilliant attorneys get sidelined—because no one ever taught them how to get clients. Not in law school. Not at the firm. It doesn't matter if you look the part or not—you can't play a game where you don't know the rules.*

*I've seen it over and over. That moment when the whisper creeps in: "I'm not bringing in enough." But no one ever says to themselves,* **"Why?"**

*That gap? It isn't personal. It's just been passed down, unexamined.*

*Rainmaker: Unleashed isn't just a book—it's a reckoning. For decades, attorneys have been told that rainmaking is an "art," a mysterious skill you either have or you don't. But here's the truth: it's not magic. It's strategy. It's relationships. And it's a learned skill—just not one the legal industry ever stopped to examine.*

*Not because those partners were trying to gatekeep. But because most partners didn't even know what they were doing.*

*You can't teach what you've never had to explain.*

*In a profession obsessed with precision and training, it's shocking how little instruction exists on the one thing that determines whether an attorney stays or goes: revenue.*

*Law firms invest in CLEs, trial advocacy workshops, and leadership programs—and yes, many say they're teaching rainmaking. But here's the issue: you can't teach what's never been deconstructed. At best, it's talked about. But it's rarely broken down into something attorneys can actually learn, apply, and own.*

*It's not intentional silence.*
*It's absence.* **Assumption. Inheritance.**

*It's the thing that was never written down, never taught, never even acknowledged.*

*Too many brilliant attorneys stall out—or burn out—not because they aren't excellent lawyers, but because no one ever showed them how client relationships are actually built.*

*And when they do ask for help, the advice is usually vague, inconsistent, or based on personal style—not strategy.*

- ✓ *"Take a law school friend to lunch."*
- ✓ *"Get out there more."*
- ✓ *"Network."*
- ✓ *"Speak on a panel."*
- ✓ *"Just ask for the work."*

*And many just wait by the phone. You think it's going to ring because a stranger's just dying to hand over a million-dollar case? Please. You have a better chance with the Lotto.*

**Rainmaker: Unleashed** *changes that.*

*It's not a script. It's not a list of tired tips recycled from 1990s sales books. It's a modern, honest, and personal conversation about how to turn relationships into revenue—without selling your soul or pretending to be someone you're not.*

*This isn't about getting attention. It's about getting clients. And unlike the books that asks you to fake confidence, perfect your elevator pitch, or enhance your golf game—this one tells the truth: real rainmaking isn't loud. It's smart.*

*This book is built on 20+ years of consulting to lawyers—first securing the right resources to win the cases they brought in, and later shaping how they approached their networks strategically.*

Rainmaker: Unleashed

*It draws from real stories, real barriers, and real breakthroughs.*

*Most importantly, it's for the attorney who's smart enough to know that being excellent at lawyering isn't enough—and is ready to play a bigger, bolder game.*

*This book exists because no one wrote it for us. And I got tired of waiting.*

*— Sejal Bhasker Patel, Founder of Sage Ivy Consulting*

# The Book I Wish Existed

Me? Writing a book like this? Hell no. I didn't even know a book like this could exist. But maybe that's exactly the point. This isn't coming from someone who always knew she'd make it. This is coming from someone who had to claw her way in, trip over the rules, and learn to break them with style.

And once I did? I realized I wasn't the only one who was never taught the rules in the first place.

You can't win a game if no one tells you how it works.
Are the people with the most power the smartest? Or just the ones who bring in the most revenue?
The account leads. The rainmakers.
How'd they get there? What's different about them—or about you?
That's the question.
The answer is *revenue*.

That's why I started Sage Ivy.
Not to "coach" people. Not to do lunch-and-learns.
I built this company because I was tired of watching brilliant attorneys get passed over—while smooth talkers with golf club memberships made partner.

If I could empower the brilliant-but-overlooked attorneys—the ones who never got the playbook but show up and deliver every time—to build relationships that actually lead to clients?

Then I could change who holds the power. ***Quietly. Strategically. Permanently.***

Rainmaking isn't just about getting credit. It's about getting a seat at the table—so you can flip the damn table when you need to.

I grew up in Lincoln, Nebraska, immigrant family. I didn't have connections. Didn't belong to a country club. Sucked at golf. While I grew up with the Cornhuskers central to our universe—I could take it or leave it. Football didn't define me.

No cheat code for me. I started the way most people do—thinking hard work was enough.

# Rainmaker: Unleashed

Let's rewind to 2003. I land a job at Navigant Consulting. What I don't know is that my boss didn't even want me interviewing in the New York office—he figured they wouldn't hire me. I found that out later, naturally. So instead, I got sent to the Princeton office. Younger group. More likely to take a shot on someone who didn't look the part.

The irony? I wouldn't have even landed in Princeton if Randy—my boss at the time—hadn't sent me. New York passed. He saw something in me and said, "Go where they'll take a shot." He was the one who told me, long before I believed it myself, "You need to start Sejal, Inc."

I didn't even know what that meant back then. Now? That seed became Sage Ivy.

They were hiring JDs to go into law firms and pitch services—damages experts, forensic accountants, PhD whiz-kids. Basically, sell the consultants without ever calling it selling. Practice development. What did that even mean? How? I didn't know the first thing about rainmaking. But I was smart. Relentless. And totally game.

Picture it: I'm thirty. An Indian woman from Nebraska. In rooms full of white male partners in their fifties. I didn't play golf. No Ivy League pedigree.

I'd read the bio like a scout—college, hometown, anything I could weaponize. Then I'd call my brother Amit for a crash course: "Give me three things about the Celtics so I don't sound like an idiot." He was basically my pre-meeting SportsCenter. I'd memorize the talking points, show up, and drop them into conversation like I knew what I was doing.

But it never landed. Not because I didn't care. It wasn't *authentic*—it wasn't me.

I didn't know how to connect with them—not in the way that builds trust. Not in the way that gets clients to want to work with you.

They handed me a playbook: memorize our accolades, spit out our value prop, hit the circuit—lunches, events, Yankees games, golf outings, steak dinners. Go where the lawyers go. Get close to power. The business will follow.

So I did it—every bit of it. Over 800 meetings in two years. No exaggeration. *Eight. Hundred.* And the total revenue I brought in? Zero.

Rainmaker: Unleashed

***Not a single damn dollar.***

I wasn't just failing—I was *invisible*. And trust me, invisible is way worse.

Then I'm at a company retreat, having a drink with John from the Chicago office. He looks at me and goes, "You've had more meetings than anyone. What the hell are you saying in them?" He wasn't criticizing. He was trying to figure out how the hell I was doing it.

So I launch into my script—the elevator pitch, the slick folders, the branding language.

He cuts me off, mid-sentence. "Stop. Just...stop. Be you."

I blink. "Me? Like, *me* me? The girl who rolls her eyes when people posture? The one who calls bullshit on, well... BS?"

"Exactly. Be *that* woman. What do you have to lose? The firm's going to fire you in six months anyway." I'd spent two years trying it their way—and now I had a six-month runway left. That night? Everything changed.

I ditched the script. No more brochures. No more stifling my soul in mundane conversations. I walked into lunches, meetings or cocktail parties and just... talked. I asked questions. Challenged people. Told the truth. Listened harder.

And guess what?

Six months later, I brought in over $6 million in revenue.

So let's get something straight: This book? It's for ***ALL of US***.

You did everything right. Checked the boxes. Hit the billables.
Built the reputation.

You're a damn good lawyer—you know your craft.
And still? Client development feels like some magic trick no one ever taught you.

The dirty secret: Law school didn't prep you for *this*. It trained you to think, write, argue. Not how to get clients. And when that moment comes—when you *have* to bring in clients—no one teaches you how.

Rainmaker: Unleashed

They just wait to see if you'll sink—or swim. Ever ask yourself why? Or how?

How'd those partners get the intro, the opportunity, the client—why not me?

If you've ever been told to "just network more," and thought, *duh, how?*

If you've ever whispered to yourself, *Maybe I'm just not cut out for this…*

Then this book is especially for you.

I observed. I studied. I started asking the "why" and the "how." I didn't get here by winging it—and I'm not handing you some paint-by-numbers formula. This isn't regurgitated advice dressed up as insight. What I'm giving you is earned. **Strategy. Perspective**. The real story of how client relationships actually happen.

For years, I sat between partners and the consultants they needed. My job? Listen to the case, assess the personalities, and match them with the right expert. Credentials mattered. But chemistry closed the deal.

I used to joke that I was the Match.com of legal consulting. No joke. That was the job. And I was damn good at it.

**I made it rain *without* a billable hour.**

Eventually—without even realizing it—I became the expert. I'd share how I followed up, how I built relationships, how I thought about client strategy... and they took notes. That's when it clicked. This wasn't common sense. It wasn't being taught. And the people around me? They were hungry for exactly what I had figured out the hard way. Years in the making—and now it crystallized: this isn't instinct. It's not obvious. It's a *skill*.

I'm not alone. No one knows how to do this.

That's why I started Sage Ivy—a company built to close the gap no one talks about.

The missing link. How to convert relationships into revenue.

I've taken everything I've learned—and turned it into a system individuals and firms can actually use to drive revenue.

The strategies inside are drawn from the same work I do with law firms through a deeper consulting series. You won't find that framework here.

What you *will* find is the philosophy, the pressure points, and the clarity that make rainmaking possible.

*If it resonates, that's not luck. That's the edge.*

Why this book? Because inside, you'll learn how to follow up without sounding desperate. How to stay seen without selling your soul. And how to turn your personality into your strategy—so you never have to fake it to make it again.

This is the book I needed at 30 when I was invisible. It's the book I wish someone had written. And now? It's the book I wrote for **all of us**.

Let's start where the gap begins.
Maybe it wasn't a lie.
Maybe you just didn't know.
**But now?**
**You will.**
**That's why this book exists.**

# Chapter 1

Rainmaker: Unleashed

# Made Partner? Now Bring in Business.

Hey, congrats on making Partner. You made it. Law school. Grueling hours as an Associate. You made it. *Phew.*

Now what?

Your actual work might stay the same—but everything around you just leveled up. There's a whole new set of expectations in your purview now. And no one's going to hand you the playbook.

Law school didn't prep you for this.

You work hard. You bill hours. You're responsive. For years, that was enough.
*Now? There's more.*

**As a Partner, you're expected to hit a number—a revenue number. Every year.**

And the part no one says out loud:
**Can you bring in clients?**

If your stomach just dropped, you're not alone.
What tools are actually provided?
What training?
What guidance?

Who are you supposed to turn to?
Where's the support for *this* part of the role?

I've seen this happen so many times. Brilliant attorneys. Exacting researchers. Strategic thinkers. People who could destroy a deposition and charm a room—but couldn't get a seat at the table because they didn't know how to turn their relationships into revenue.

*And they didn't know they were supposed to.*

Here's the conundrum. You're trained to be an excellent attorney. You're rewarded for being thorough, accurate, and smart. You panels. You sat with clients. But you never quite saw how the dough was made. ***Each. And. Every. step.*** of bringing in a client.

That skillset—the one that will eventually determine whether you rise, plateau, or leave—is treated like a bonus. Like an optional elective. Until it's suddenly required.

And by then? The people who've quietly figured it out are already miles ahead.

## The Pyramid No One Talks About

Law firms are pyramids, structurally and strategically. This isn't a cynical take—it's just the truth. They hire large associate classes with the full knowledge that many will burn out, wash out, or opt out before ever getting near partnership.

But even when you make it to "Partner," the word doesn't always mean what you think it means.

*Let's be real:* there's no such thing as a "junior partner" title in the legal system. The formal title is just "Partner." But inside most firms, the distinctions are very real.

Junior partners may control origination.

But most firms never break down how origination credit is structured—or how to grow it.

You'll hear people say, "He's non-equity," meaning, there are still more metrics to be met before you go up the ladder and become an Equity Partner. That's the inner circle of the firm.

*You're in—but you're not yet in.*

## You Don't Get Pulled. You Get Left Off.

You won't get pulled off pitches. That's not how it works. You just might never get invited in the first place.

If you've built strong internal relationships—especially with senior partners—you'll get pulled in, mentored, and sponsored. But if you haven't? If you've been head-down, excellent, and invisible? You're on your own.

*And no one tells you that.*

The same goes for panels, client dinners, speaking opportunities. None of it's behind a locked door—*but it is sealed behind a knowledge gap.* Marketing might be too busy focusing on the firm's marquee rainmakers. Leadership isn't going to hand-feed you a strategy. If you want to be visible, you have to figure it out.

*But again—no one says that out loud.*

## The Joke That Wasn't a Joke

There was a running joke that partners didn't know the associates' names. We all laughed—but I still wonder if that was ever really a joke.

**A lot of people are invisible.**

Unless you were loud, charming, or naturally political—your "the work speaks for itself" philosophy is great in theory. But in reality? It sucks.

Say you speak up, if you weren't already part of someone's internal circle, it doesn't mean you'd be remembered.

That invisibility doesn't vanish when you make partner. It just becomes quieter. You've got about a two-year runway to hit your numbers. To figure it out. If not? Start updating your résumé. That's why most attorneys leave—and suddenly, retention becomes a firm-wide priority.

## The Truth About Training

Some firms try to train you. They'll put on a rainmaking session. They'll assign you a mentor. They might even bring in an outside coach for a 90-minute presentation on "building your brand." But those efforts, while well-intentioned, often miss the mark.

*Here's why.*

Senior partners often can't explain what they never had to consciously learn. They say things like, "Just stay visible," "Keep your name top of mind," "Be the go-to."

The part they skip? *How* to become that person.

Because most of them never had to reverse-engineer it. They were invited into relationships. Handed books. Shown the way.

And outside coaches? Many of them have never worked in law. They don't understand the pressures of the billable hour. They don't understand the politics of origination. They don't understand the grind of staying top-tier *and* trying to generate revenue. The delicate balance of the billable hour and client acquisition.

They show up with templates, buzzwords, and sales language that doesn't always translate. One of my clients once told me, "The coach helped me put language to what I already did." And he's right—he's a natural rainmaker. He didn't need the training.

But there's a difference between giving someone the words and giving them the strategy. ***Words describe behavior. Strategy turns it into power.***

But if you're not a natural? Those sessions don't show you how to build. They just hand you the language and hope it clicks.

And when it doesn't, you're left thinking everyone else got the manual—and you missed the first chapter.

## The Ones Who Slip Away

I had a law school friend, Dan, who made partner. He was smart, well-liked, an excellent lawyer. Not enough. He couldn't bring in clients. He tried. And eventually, he left to go in-house.

At the time, I didn't know how to help him. I hadn't figured this out yet myself. But now, looking back, I know: it wasn't him. It was the system.

He got the title, but not the strategy. He was expected to swim without ever being taught how to tread water. And when he didn't? The firm let him go quietly—and kept whatever client relationships he'd helped develop along the way.

He took a job in-house. It was stable, respectable. But it capped him. That move put a ceiling on his earnings he'll probably never break through.

The firm? They kept growing off the foundation he helped build. He walked away with a paycheck. They kept the pipeline.

I wish I knew then what I know now. I could've helped him build it. I could've shown him how to think about conversations, relationships, triggers, follow-ups. I could've given him the confidence to own his space.

Instead, he became one of many who slipped through.

**And here's the part no one talks about:**
Dan isn't an outlier. He's the blueprint.
Talented. Reliable. Liked.
But once the rules changed, no one gave him the playbook.

The system assumes that making Partner means you suddenly know how to get clients. And when you don't? It moves on without blinking.

This isn't just a BigLaw playbook. If your clients are individuals—founders, families, plaintiffs—you're still rainmaking. You just play on a different field. The same core principles apply: trust, visibility, loyalty. But your strategy might look different.

Maybe you're building trust with financial planners and accountants who funnel referrals your way. Maybe you're giving CLEs or community presentations that position you as the go-to for high-net-worth families. Maybe you need a system that keeps your network warm without a marketing department behind you.

That's still rainmaking. But most attorneys in that world never get told that—so they write themselves out of the game before they've even started.

We don't just lose good lawyers that way. We lose future leaders. And then firms wonder why retention's such a problem. That's why I built a framework to help attorneys not just stay—but lead.

## Why Most Advice Falls Flat

Most business development training gives you tactics, not tools. A list of things to try, not a way to think. It sounds helpful—until you're back at your desk wondering what the hell to actually *do*.

You've probably heard some version of this before:

**Go to events**
**Send follow-up emails**
**Post on LinkedIn**
**"Build rapport"**
**"Be more visible"**

But what does rapport even mean? And how do you become "more visible" when you've been taught your whole career to keep your head down and just do excellent work? It's all vague without the *how*.

I work with a lot of introverted attorneys. They're brilliant at what they do. But the second the conversation moves away from work—their legal expertise—they freeze. They're afraid of small talk. Afraid of being awkward. Afraid of saying the wrong thing. They don't know how to build trust unless they're discussing the case.

So when I work with them, I break it down into small, specific steps. I tell them what to say. I give them ideas for topics that feel authentic. I remind them that talking about their favorite vacation or what they're watching on Netflix is still relationship building.

Because rapport isn't about being charming—it's about being human.

*And that's the piece no one teaches.*

### *If You've Been Quietly Panicking—You're Not Alone*

If you've felt that rising panic—"I should know how to do this. Why don't I?"—let me say this as clearly as I can:

You weren't supposed to already know this.
Most attorneys aren't taught how to build client relationships—not because anyone's withholding the information, but because it's never really been broken down.

## This Isn't Just About Law

*To be clear—this book may speak to attorneys, but the strategies inside work for anyone who wants to get better at building real relationships.* Swap "client" for "customer." Replace "referral" with "recommendation." It still works. Because this isn't about law firms. It's about how trust is built, how reputations are earned, and how connection becomes your power.

If you're reading this thinking, *"I should've figured this out by now"*— you're not behind.
You've just stepped into the part of your career no one ever explained.

*This book is the roadmap that should've always existed.*
*And it starts right here.*

# Chapter 2

# Not All Rainmakers Look Alike

Everyone loves a "natural," right? The golden child. The one who swaggers into a networking event and walks out with three business cards, two lunch meetings, and a potential panel spot. The partner who "just knows" how to work a room. The one everyone points to and says, "Now that's a rainmaker."

*Is it?*

Here's the truth no one says out loud:
*Showy guy might not be a rainmaker at all.*
He's just doing what he thinks he has to do to be successful.

## The Illusion of the "Type"

There's a certain image that tends to show up when people talk about rainmakers. They're extroverted, confident, socially fluent—the kind of person who seems to know everyone and gets invited everywhere. Golf outings, conference panels, dinners with the managing partner. They're not just doing the work—they're visible. They're out there. They're seen.

And when that's the only version of success that gets spotlighted, it messes with your head. You start to wonder if that's the only way to play this game.

What if you're not built like that?

What if you're great one-on-one but awkward in big rooms?

What if small talk makes your skin crawl and you'd rather ask deep questions than toss around banter?

It's easy to start thinking, *Maybe this just isn't for me.*

But that's not a personal failure. That's a missing translation. No one ever showed you what this could look like on your terms—so you assumed you were doing it wrong.

## The Charisma Myth

Some people make it look easy.

They walk into a room and immediately know who to talk to. Their stories land. Their timing's perfect. They're funny, confident, polished. It seems effortless. And because it looks natural, we assume it is.

They get labeled "the naturals." The ones you point to and think, *They're just wired for this.*

But here's what no one tells you: most "natural rainmakers" can't explain what they do.

Ask them how they connect with clients, and the answers are vague.

"Just be yourself."
"Get out there more."
"People either like you or they don't."

That kind of advice doesn't help the partner who shuts down the second the topic isn't legal. It doesn't help the associate who's sharp, thoughtful, and strategic—but freezes when it's time to make small talk or transition to relationship-building.

***Because charisma isn't a strategy. It's a style.***

And rainmaking isn't about style—it's about structure. What to say. When to follow up. How to build trust without sounding like a pitch deck.

You don't need to be magnetic. You just need to be intentional. That's where strategy comes in.

***Rainmaking isn't about instinct. It's not magic. It's intention—and it's learned.***

## What Clients Actually Want

Clients don't want to be dazzled. They want to feel understood. They want to trust you with their risk. They want to believe you can make their lives easier—and their outcomes stronger.

And above all? *They want you to make them look good.*

Lawyers often think subject-matter expertise is what earns loyalty. But as Paul Grewal, Chief Legal Officer at Coinbase, once said—it's not about proving you're the smartest. It's about showing up when it matters and understanding what's at stake.

You don't need to be loud to make someone feel safe. You need to listen. Ask smart questions. Show up consistently. And follow up in a way that builds momentum—without making it awkward or transactional.

That's not personality. That's process.

*And process can be taught.*

## Building a Bridge, Not Faking a Spark

One of my clients—let's call him Jack—is an exceptional attorney. Brilliant on substance, composed under pressure, and deeply thoughtful. But when conversations drifted outside legal work—into rapport, follow-up, or small talk—he froze.

Not because he didn't care. But because no one had ever shown him how to do it in a way that felt natural.

So we started small.

We didn't change his personality. We gave it a framework.

We walked through what to say in those early moments—how to ease into rapport with topics that felt genuine, not forced. Then we moved into deeper questions. Not just, "What's new at work?" but conversations that uncovered what actually mattered to the client—professionally and personally. Goals. Growth. Pains they weren't naming.

With each interaction, Jack had structure. He wasn't winging it anymore. He was prepared. And that structure gave him confidence.

It turned freak-out moments into connection points.

That's the shift.

*We didn't make him a different person. We just gave him control.*

We get this wrong outside of law too.

My brother, Samir, calls the shots for our family businesses. He's charismatic. He's the guy everyone knows—and somehow, he knows everything about everyone around him. Where they went on vacation. Who just had surgery. Which vendor's daughter just got into college. He remembers the details, and he always checks in—even when there's nothing in it for him.

On the surface, he looks like a "natural."
But the truth is—he's intentional. Strategic. Consistent.
He doesn't wing it. He works it. And that's why people trust him.

This doesn't just apply to BigLaw. It applies to any field where people make decisions based on trust.

## Don't Switch Hats—Blend Them

A lot of attorneys put on different caps. There's the "work" version—precise, composed, credible. And then there's the "personal" version—funny, sarcastic, warm. But when it comes to client development, they don't realize the best relationships are built in the overlap.

It's not about switching hats. It's about letting you be a big, beautiful mess.

That's what makes it real.

Clients don't want a curated version of you. They want the one who can talk about the deal *and* ask about their kid's soccer tournament. *That blend? That's where authenticity lives.*

And that's what makes people want to come back to you.

## Visibility Isn't the Same as Value

Some people get noticed early. Maybe they're charismatic. Maybe they talk a lot. Maybe they just happened to be in the right room at the right time. They get invited to more panels. Pulled into pitches. Given a shot. And suddenly, they're seen as "the rainmaker."

But that visibility isn't the same as skill. And it definitely isn't the same as strategy. Just because someone's visible doesn't mean they're doing it well. It just means they got picked—and once you get picked, it's easier to stay picked. That's how the myth builds.

And everyone else? They start to feel behind. Or broken. Like they're missing a chip.

They're not.

*They're just missing the rule book.*

You don't need to copy whatever version of success your firm keeps holding up. You don't need to become a 'natural.' *You need to be authentic—and build a strategy that actually fits you.*

# Chapter 3

# Your Network Isn't Flat—It's Untapped

*When I started doing business development, I thought I had to meet new people constantly.* Conferences. Cocktail parties. Dinners. I was everywhere. My contact list exploded—but nothing moved.

It wasn't until I stopped chasing strangers and looked at who I already knew that everything changed. My first real streak of momentum didn't come from new names. It came from *reconnections*.

*Biggest mistake I see attorneys make?* They treat their network like a spreadsheet. Linear. Passive. Dead—or even ignored.

But your network isn't flat. It's layered. Dynamic. Alive. And most of its power? You're not even touching it—*because no one taught you how.* There's strategy behind it.

## The Myth of "More"

Lawyers love more. More credentials. More experience. More CLEs. So when it comes to rainmaking, the instinct is the same: "I need to meet more people."

**Dead Wrong.**

What you need is to look at your current network *differently*.

Most attorneys already know hundreds of people—clients, former classmates, opposing counsel, bar association contacts, law school friends, even that woman you met once on a panel who still follows you on LinkedIn.

*Here's the thing*: no one tells you how to *work* that network. How to move from acquaintance to conversation. From helpful to trusted. From connected to paid.

## The Relationship Pyramid

Think of your network like a pyramid:

At the top? Your **power contacts.** These are people who trust you and can refer or hire today. Folks you can text and grab a drink with. These are your go-to people—the ones who return your call without needing a calendar invite.

In the middle? Your **warm relationships**—the people who like you but don't fully understand what you do. These are the connections you haven't reconnected with since the pandemic, the colleagues you see at industry events but never really follow up with, the ones who could become clients or connectors if you reached out with purpose.

At the bottom? Everyone else—former colleagues, law school classmates, loose connections you've never followed up with.

*Here's the secret:* most people try to build from the bottom up. You don't have to. You **start in the middle.** That's where the energy is.

The trust is already halfway built. You're not convincing strangers—you're reactivating relationships that just need a reason to reengage. And they're closer to converting than you think.

## Stop Looking for Cold Intros

Everyone wants to meet the GC of a major company. But you don't start there. You build toward it. And sometimes? That GC you're trying to reach… is already two degrees away in your current network. You just haven't mapped it. And if you don't map it, you'll keep chasing strangers while your actual network sits untouched.

Lawyers are trained to analyze. But when it comes to relationships, they rely on memory or instinct instead of actual structure. That's where the opportunity gets lost. You'd never build a case based on guesswork—so why treat your network that way?

You don't need 50 new contacts. You need to **sort, prioritize, and re-engage** the ones you already have.

## Weaving It In—Not Adding It On

Don't overhaul everything. You're already overloaded. This isn't about adding—it's about weaving. Making relationship-building part of how you move through your day. Like how you prep for a hearing or manage billables—intentional, seamless, and rooted in who you already are.

Pick a few people each week who bring you energy or curiosity. Reach out. No pitch. No agenda. Just a connection that keeps the relationship alive.

That's how it started with Beth.

We were co-workers, but I didn't trust her. To be honest, I don't usually trust anyone I work with.

Then one year, we were at a conference in Florida and the NYC airports got snowed in. Flights canceled. Everyone panicked.

We ended up stuck an extra day—and somehow, at the spa together.

That was the first time I let my guard down. No panels. No posturing. Just—two women exhaling.

That one day changed everything. Beth's now my rock. Not because we worked together—but because we *connected*.

And it never would've happened if I hadn't stopped hiding behind the idea that work and real friendship can't mix.

## Contact List to Strategy

Once you've given yourself permission to reconnect, the next step is *clarity*.

This is where most attorneys get stuck. You know people. You've built relationships over the years. But you've never turned that into an actual plan. And it's not because you're lazy—it's because no one's ever shown you how to treat your network like something you can shape.

You don't need to send mass emails. You just need a quiet strategy for staying in touch with people in a way that feels authentic and sustainable.

*Clarity kills hesitation. Get sharp on these three things:*

- ✓ Who's already in your orbit

- ✓ What kind of relationship you actually want to build
- ✓ What light touch keeps you visible without being awkward

And don't underestimate the digital tools staring you in the face. LinkedIn—when you actually use it—can keep you top of mind with people you haven't talked to since 2019. No emails. No cold outreach. Just quiet visibility. But that only works if your network's actually in there—and not sitting in some forgotten spreadsheet from your last job.

You don't have to do it all at once. You start with the people who already know your name—and just need a reason to remember why.

## Why You've Ignored the Good Ones

You know why most people don't follow up with the warm contacts in their network? *Because there's shame.*

You think: "I haven't talked to her in 3 years." "It's probably too late now." "She probably already has a lawyer."

*That internal script? It's garbage.*

People don't sit around judging you for not reaching out sooner. They're busy. Just like you. And when you show up with relevance, warmth, or value, they're not annoyed—they're relieved.

## A True Story of Reconnection

One of my clients hadn't reached out to an old contact in four years. They'd worked on a deal together and hadn't talked since.

She almost didn't send the email. She felt uncomfortable about the gap.

I gave her a sentence. Just one:
*"I was thinking about the work we did together and realized how long it's been—I'd love to catch up and hear what you're working on."*

In that moment, she wasn't pitching. She wasn't angling. She was **resurrecting the relationship** and **taking interest**—and that changed everything.

Rainmaker: Unleashed

Thirty minutes later, the reply came in.
Lunch was set.
Three weeks later? Referral.
Two months later? Client.

Besides, it can't hurt to try. Why are you reading this otherwise?

## Seen ≠ Chosen

You know who gets referred? The people who are top of mind. You know who gets passed over? The ones who quietly crush it—but never check in. Ask your client how they pick their lawyer. You might think it's about credentials. But it's usually about who showed up last.

Rainmaking isn't about being the best. It's about being known to be the best—by the right people, *at the right time.*

And most attorneys? They think they're being "polite" by not following up. But really, they're stuck in an old mindset—waiting for the phone to ring. **That world is over.**

You can't sit back and hope to be remembered. That's how you stay a commodity. If you want to be a trusted advisor, you have to show up like one.

## The Ask That Kills Momentum

One of my clients told me that a senior partner once advised him to just say:
*"What's it going to take to win your business?"*

That's the kind of line that might sound good in a sales seminar—but in real life, it lands wrong. Especially for women.

Can you imagine asking a male GC that question over lunch? The implications. The power imbalance. The tone. It's awkward at best—and professionally dangerous at worst.

And beyond that, it gives you the ICK. Especially for younger partners and associates—women feel it even more. No one wants to be the used car salesperson of the legal industry.

That kind of move puts all the pressure on them—and makes it ALL about what you want, not what they need.

## The Rings of Relevance

Not all relationships carry the same weight—and not every connection deserves the same kind of follow-up.

To make it manageable (and honest), I have attorneys sort them into rings. Here's how I have attorneys think about their relationships:

- ✓ *Ride-Or-Dies* – the friendships. The ones you can call without a second thought and end up at drinks after work.

- ✓ *Shoulda Texted* – the ones you genuinely like, but it's just been too long. Maybe it's been… forever. No drama. Just life.

- ✓ *Hmm… Can't Remember* – the vague connections. People you met at a conference or bar event and genuinely don't remember, but you know they're on your phone.

I once sat in a bar with a BigLaw partner I used to work with—let's call him Dick. We spent five hours going through his contact list. I'm talking old clients, forgotten connections, random business school names he hadn't thought about in years.

We looked at each one—who had power, who needed a warm-up, who was worth a reintroduction. I helped him reshape how he thought about outreach, how to prioritize, and what kind of ask would land. This wasn't guesswork. It was strategic.

He landed a $2 million Goldman deal from that napkin session.

*And that's when it clicked for me:*

Even the Ivy League BigLaw partner—the résumé, the pedigree, the $1,500/hour rate—were taking notes from me.

Relationships don't run on pedigree. They run on pattern recognition. Strategy. Movement.

*Rainmaker: Unleashed*

That's when I learned what I thought was common sense… wasn't common. Most attorneys need a flashlight. Turns out, I'd been carrying one for years—I just didn't realize it had a switch.

## The Trust Timeline

Most people stop at "great to meet you." But trust isn't built in one interaction. It takes repeated *relevance. Consistency. Thoughtfulness.*

Rainmakers don't just say hello. They know how to keep the conversation going long after the handshake.

***Secret Sauce:*** *it takes **7 to 8 meaningful interactions** to convert relationships into revenue.*

We'll dig deeper into how to build that kind of momentum later in the book.

## Relationships Are Not One-Directional

Something no one likes to admit: a lot of attorneys hoard their contacts—not just from competitors, but from their own colleagues. They avoid entering relationships into the firm's CRM system. Why? Because deep down, they know the relationship isn't strong enough to withstand someone else stepping in.

*The truth*: if the relationship was solid, it wouldn't be at risk. No one can "steal" a client who actually trusts you. You're a commodity and easily replaceable.

Instead of protecting weak ties, what if you focused on strengthening them? Instead of keeping contacts siloed, what if you made yourself indispensable?

Because rainmaking isn't about possession.
It's about movement.
***Visibility.***
***Trust.***
***Longevity.***

Think of your network like puzzle pieces. You might not always be the missing piece yourself—but sometimes you're the one who can connect two people who complete something bigger. A secondment. A board seat. A next job. A personal intro that changes their entire year.

And have you ever actually asked your current clients what they need?

Not legal work—support. *Openings. Insight. Access.*

*Questions like:*

- ✓ "What are your personal goals?"
- ✓ "What are your professional goals this year?"
- ✓ "How else can I help you?"

That's the stuff that sticks. That's what moves you from lawyer… to **trusted advisor.**

The person they trust with their biggest asks, their most sensitive problems—even what restaurant to book for their anniversary dinner. Because once they trust you with the personal? They'll trust you with the professional, too.

You don't have to be everywhere. You just have to be intentional with the people already in your orbit.

In the next chapter, we'll talk about how to follow up in a way that feels natural—*not needy*—and how momentum dies when you let your connections go cold.

# Chapter 4

# Conversations Aren't One-Night Stands

*My father once tried to launch a company with a first-generation computer.* He had the guts, the brains, and the vision. But he partnered with a sales guy who couldn't sell. The company failed.

Later, my dad told me something that never left me: *"The product is replaceable. The knowledge is replaceable. But the ability to get clients? That's the hard part."*
That one line rewired my brain.

*That line shaped everything that came after.* I went to law school thinking it would open every door. Prestige, power, purpose—whatever I thought was waiting on the other side. But here's what no one told me: law school teaches you how to think like a lawyer. *It does not teach you how to get clients.*

*And follow-up?* That's the part where most people fumble the client they didn't even know they had in their hands.

## The Energy Dies in Silence

You meet someone at a conference. Great conversation. You connect on LinkedIn. And then—*crickets.* No follow-up. No value-add. No next move. The energy flatlines.

Then, three months later, you see that same person speaking on a panel— next to your colleague. From your firm.

This is how it slips away—quietly, without you even knowing you lost it.

Not because you weren't impressive. Not because they didn't like you. But because you didn't stay visible. Because in the absence of follow-up, the connection didn't deepen. The energy just…*died.*

*Most attorneys treat follow-up like a chore.* Send the thank-you. Set the calendar ping. Loop back with a "just checking in" a month later. But that's not follow-up—that's box-checking. That's if they even do any follow up at all.

Real follow-up isn't transactional. It's not a template. It's how you stay relevant, stay remembered, and stay trusted.

*Here's the truth*: if the only thing you ever talked about was work? If you never got past the resume or the billable topic? Then yeah—follow-up sucks. It feels awkward. Forced.

But if you actually connected—if you saw the human, not just the title? Then it's easy. You're texting them a restaurant rec. Asking how their son's soccer game went. Following up about that Beyoncé concert they mentioned. That's not a strategy. That's a relationship.

## Start With Interest, Not the Ask

Follow-up isn't about pushing. It's about presence. And if you want to stay present? Stay curious—or risk being forgettable.

Lead with interest—but start from the beginning. Where did they grow up? Did they always live in this city? Where did they go to school? Learn who they are before diving into what they do. Once you've earned that familiarity, then ask: What are they working on? What's changing in their industry? What's keeping them up at night? Because the most meaningful follow-up starts with knowing the person, not just their title.

When the relationship is real, you won't have to ask. **The opportunity finds you**.

## A Structure for the People Who Need It

Not everyone is naturally outgoing. I work with brilliant attorneys who crush it in the courtroom—but freeze the second the conversation shifts away from work. If it's not about a case or statute, they go blank. No clue what to say. No idea how to pivot.

**Don't wing it. Build structure:**

- ✓ Start with something personal—where they're from, how they got into their field, what they do for fun. Build a real foundation. Watch how they talk when they're relaxed—not performing. Ask open-ended questions that show you're actually listening. Then, once you've earned that comfort, ease into the work stuff: what's new, what's changing, what's taking up their headspace. Most of the time? They'll ask you what you do before you even have to bring it up.

- ✓ Ease into it. Don't lead with "So what are your goals?"—you'll sound like a spreadsheet. Instead, get curious about how they got here. Ask things like, "Did you always think you'd end up in this field?" or "What pulled you into this work?" Keep it casual. Make it feel like you're just talking—not collecting intel. And when they relax? That's when they tell you what actually matters.

- ✓ By this point, if you've actually been paying attention, you already know how to be helpful. You've asked the right questions. You've learned what matters. Now you show up with something relevant—*not generic*. That's what makes you unforgettable.

That's it. That's the play. Sounds simple, right? Try it. You'll learn more about yourself than you expected. It's like lifting weights for the first time—awkward, uncomfortable, maybe even a little embarrassing. But that's how you get stronger. That's how you grow.

You don't need to memorize a pitch. In fact, I get asked about elevator pitches all the time—and I hate them. Don't you? What makes you memorable isn't a polished 30-second summary of your practice. It's the human stuff. The way you made them laugh. The story you told about your family. That moment you both joked that *age is just a number*. The connection that stuck. No one is hiring you based on what you say in 30 seconds. They're hiring you because they trust you. So be curious, attentive, and consistent—and dump the elevator pitch.

## Following Up After a Long Silence

I once worked with a partner named Mark—sharp, introverted, and incredibly thoughtful. He told me about a former colleague, Sue, who had gone in-house a few years earlier. They'd been Associates together. But life got busy. Work took over. And they lost touch.

Mark sent her an email:
*"Sue—it's been a while, but you popped into my head the other day and I thought we should grab lunch and see what's happening in your life."*

No grand plan. Just one lunch.
And that's all it took.

That one lunch turned into a series of conversations. A few months later, she referred him work. Not because he asked—but because he showed up as himself. *Authentic.*

You don't need to over-explain the gap. Just reach out. Most relationships aren't dead—they're just *dormant*. Waiting to be reopened.

## Follow-Up by Personality: How You're Wired Affects How You Show Up

Follow-up isn't one-size-fits-all. How you're wired shows up. And it matters more than you think. I've seen this play out with clients, over and over again.

*Introverts* tend to need more structure. When I ask them about a meeting, I have to walk them through it—step by step: *"Then what happened?" "How did they react?" "What was their body language?"*

They make me work to help them help themselves. They get stuck in their own heads, overthinking every word. Follow-up feels daunting because they're not sure what to say—or how to ask questions that actually reveal who someone is.

*Extroverts*, on the other hand? Never short on words. They give me *every* detail—and then some. The challenge isn't pulling information from them—it's getting them to pause. To listen. Extroverts struggle with follow-up because they're already planning the next story. I have to teach them to slow down. To actually observe. To stay curious, not just entertaining.

See, the myth is that rainmakers are born extroverts. That they just *know* how to work a room. But that's not what makes someone great at follow-up. The magic isn't in being charming. It's in being intentional.

The good news: *both types get better*. Once they start using the structure I lay out, the light bulb goes on. They learn how to tune into themselves. And suddenly? Follow-up isn't awkward or overwhelming anymore. It's just another way to build trust.

# The Best Follow-Up Isn't a Calendar Reminder

It's a rhythm. You stay visible. You stay useful. You stay human.

Sometimes that means texting them about the new musical they mentioned. Or sending the inside joke about pickleball you both cracked up over. Or that TV show you talked about. Then, when the timing's right, sure—send the article or forward the opportunity. But only *after* you've built a real connection. Sometimes, it's just a simple check-in: *"Hey, you crossed my mind."*

**The biggest win: You're the name that pops into their head—right when it matters.**

That's rainmaking. Not magic. Not manipulation. Just steady, relevant connection.
The goal isn't to be clever or convincing—it's to become a trusted advisor.
Someone they turn to for everything from restaurant recs to real decisions.
Not because you're pushy. Because you're present.
And that? That's the part no one can steal.
You bring something to the table no one else has—*YOU.*

Up to now, we've been focused on the people already in your orbit—the ones you've met before, and how to stay visible with relevance and authenticity.

Walk into a room full of strangers—and everything shifts. Whether it's a conference, a CLE, a bar event, or a cocktail party, it's the same challenge in a different container: *How do you connect without feeling fake? How do you stand out without selling?*

And what we're about to walk through?
It applies to any of those arenas.
Not just conferences.
Galas. Fundraisers. Women's events. CLEs. Even that random rooftop cocktail hour you said yes to at the last minute.
Wherever people gather, this strategy travels.

That's where we're headed next. Not just event tips—*real tools* for showing up sharp, strategic, and unforgettable in any room, with anyone.

# Chapter 5

# Pack Strategy, Not Just Business Cards

So far, we've focused on the people already in your orbit—your current network, the ones you've met before, and how to stay visible with relevance and authenticity.

But what happens when you walk into a room full of strangers?

Whether it's a conference, a CLE, a bar event, or a cocktail party—Same challenge, different arena: *How do you connect without feeling fake? How do you stand out without selling?*

I remember the first time I went to a conference with zero tools. I didn't know a single person. I checked into the hotel, walked over to the registration table, picked up my badge, and thought—*okay, now what?* Everyone seemed to know each other. I felt like the odd one out.

Thoughts were flying through my head: *Should I go to a session? I'm here to meet people—how do I even start? What do I say? Will anyone even talk to me or will they just walk away?* I was completely overwhelmed. None of it felt natural. It felt like walking into a giant inside joke I didn't know the punchline to.

This isn't fluff. This is strategy. That's why we're going deep.

We're not just talking event tips—we're talking strategy. The kind that makes you unforgettable in a room. Over the next few chapters, we'll break down how to navigate professional gatherings, with a deep dive into conferences—because that's where so many attorneys get stuck.

## How to Prepare Like a Rainmaker—Not a Robot

And not in a cheesy, "review the agenda and pack business cards" kind of way.

This chapter is about the real work before the room: *the thinking, the strategy, the recon, and the headspace.* Because when attorneys tell me they're bad at conferences, what they actually mean is: *I walked in cold.*

You wouldn't show up to court without prep. You wouldn't pitch a client without context. So why would you walk into one of the most opportunity-rich rooms of your year without a plan?

You can't wing it. Not if you want to turn that room into revenue.

In this chapter, we'll break down:

- ✓ How to research people before you meet them (and what to do with that info)
- ✓ How to start warming up the room before you ever arrive
- ✓ The mindset shift that makes walking into a room less terrifying
- ✓ And the strategic moves that turn a contact list into real conversations

Let's go.

## Real Prep = Recon

What's prep? ...your outfits, business cards? Nah, but with *people*.

I tell my clients all the time: research people like you're building a case file. Not to impress them—but to prepare yourself.

Before any conference, make a list of who's attending. This might come from the event page, the speaker list, or even LinkedIn posts about the event. Cross-reference the attendee list with your own network. Are any of your connections also going? Have they been before? Do they know anyone you should meet?

Then go deeper. Who do you actually want to meet, and *why*? Look them up on LinkedIn—not to stalk, but to observe. What's their tone? What do they post about? What kind of language do they use? Do they speak at conferences? Do they seem more formal or relaxed? Are they someone who comments and engages, or someone who broadcasts and disappears?

You're not collecting facts. You're listening for *voice*. You're watching for cues. You're figuring out what kind of energy they bring so you can decide how you want to approach them—*or if you even want to*.

And don't just stop at the professional headline. Scan their "About" section, scroll through old posts, see if they've written articles, been quoted, or attended other events. Sometimes you'll find gold in the personal tidbits: a post about their dog, a picture at a concert, a shoutout to their paralegal. Those are your *inroads*—the human things you can reference without sounding forced. This isn't just for conferences. It's for every lunch, every cocktail party, every "quick intro" someone sets up. If you're walking in blind, that's on you.

This is how you make sure the people you want to meet feel like *people*, not just names on a badge. This is how you walk in with clarity—and walk out remembered.

Think of it like a mock trial back in law school. You never asked a question unless you already knew the answer. That's how you should prep here, too. If you learn through research that someone has a dog, ask, "Do you have any pets?" You already know the answer, but it opens the door with ease. It sounds simple, maybe even underhanded—but when used with sincerity, it breaks the ice fast.

Just don't be fake. If you hate dogs, don't talk about dogs. Find something else that actually sparks your interest. The goal is to lead with something real, something human, and something *you* care about too. That's what makes the connection stick.

## Warm the Room Before You Get There

Most people show up at conferences thinking the first connection happens in the room. It doesn't. If you wait until you're on-site to start building momentum, you're already behind.

The warm-up begins the week—or even two weeks—before.

Start by engaging online. If you know certain people are going to be there, like or comment on one of their recent posts. Send a message saying, "Hey—I saw you're speaking at the conference next week. Looking forward to your panel." You're not asking for a meeting. You're making yourself visible in a natural, no-pressure way.

Post something on LinkedIn about the event. Mention why you're excited to attend. If you're on a panel, share it. If you're going solo, say that too. Use hashtags for the conference, tag speakers or firms if it feels authentic. Let people see that you're coming and that you're someone worth watching for.

Rainmaker: Unleashed

These small signals do two things: they make you feel more familiar when you meet in person, and they take the edge off that first awkward conversation.

And if there are people you really want to meet? Send a quick, casual message a few days before: "I saw you'll be at [Conference Name]—would love to say a quick hello if we cross paths." That's it. No pitch. No pressure.

But now they've seen your name, your face, your tone. You're not cold anymore. You're familiar.

And if it feels right? It's okay to say, "Would love to grab a coffee and hear what else you're working on." It's low-key, no pressure, and keeps the door open to connect deeper if the moment presents itself.

Rainmakers don't show up and hope to get lucky. They show up to rooms they've already started warming up from the outside.

I had a client who wasn't a natural at conferences—especially massive ones. He was headed to an event with over 25,000 people. He was overwhelmed. But the conference had an app where you could look up other attendees and send messages. He followed my advice and sent short, direct notes to people he thought he'd click with: "Hey, looks like we're both from Texas and work in similar areas. Would be great to connect for coffee or a drink—looking forward to the event."

After the conference, he told me something that stuck: "I wish I'd sent more of those. That was the key. The people I messaged were the ones I actually had real conversations with."

It wasn't a perfect script. It was just human. That's what warms up the room—and sets you apart before you ever arrive.

## Shift Your Mindset—You Belong in This Room

Let's talk about the mental game.

Too many attorneys walk into conferences feeling like outsiders. They assume the room is full of insiders, people who already know each other, who already have the clients, who already belong.

That's a lie.

The people in that room are just people. Some are figuring it out like you. Some are awkward. Some are scanning the crowd hoping someone says hi. The only difference between the ones who leave with connections and the ones who don't?

The ones who connect *decided* they belonged—before anyone else did. They didn't wait to be noticed. They walked in like their name was already on the damn banner.

That's not ego. That's presence.
You're not a guest here. You're the one they didn't know they were waiting for.

So stop circling the buffet table. Walk in like they're lucky you showed up.
Because if you're in it—you're meant to be in it. You're meant to own it.

**Preparation and presence.**

You don't need to be the most charming. You don't need to be the loudest. But you do need to own the fact that you're there for a reason—and that reason is valid.

Say it to yourself if you need to: *I belong in this room.*

The confidence doesn't come first. The showing up does.
*Confidence follows proximity.*

You don't fake it—you rehearse it.
You run through the mindset before you ever step into the room.
That way, when you walk in, it's not new—it's practiced.
You take a breath, scan the room, and move like someone who knows they bring value—because you do.

You're not faking confidence.
You're practicing ownership.

In the next chapter, we're going to talk about how to move with intention, how to start real conversations, and how to make sure people remember *you*—not just your firm name.

# Chapter 6

# Walk In With a Plan, Not a Panic Attack

Early in my career, I flew to DC to meet with Kevin—a big-deal partner I really wanted to impress. I did the prep. I read the cases. I reviewed the firm's wins. But there was one little problem: I was hungover.

I walked into his office, sat down across from him, and within two minutes, I mispronounced the name of a major case. Kevin, politely but firmly, corrected me. And I *froze*. My brain short-circuited. I nodded, stumbled through a few more awkward lines, and the meeting ended faster than I could recover. I walked out feeling like an idiot.

Years later, we ended up becoming good friends. We laugh about it now. But at the time? That moment gutted me.

And it wasn't because I didn't do the work. It's because I didn't walk in with a *mental game plan*. ***I had data—but no direction.***

You've done the research. You've warmed up the room. You've got the mindset. But let's be honest—none of that matters if you walk in on day one and immediately feel overwhelmed.

This chapter is about your *mental game plan*—the strategic blueprint you create *before* you ever pack your suitcase. Because walking into a room without a plan is how most smart, capable people lose their edge.

This isn't about mapping every moment. It's about having just enough structure so you don't freeze, flail, or end up hiding behind your phone pretending to check email.

We're going to build your pre-conference strategy—your own personalized operating system. So when you step into that lobby, you're not thinking, *"What should I be doing?"* You're thinking, *"Let's execute."*

In this chapter, we'll break down:

- ✓ How to define your personal conference goals.

- ✓ Why anchor meetings change everything.

Rainmaker: Unleashed

- ✓ How to use tools like the conference app to your advantage.

- ✓ And how to build your first-day flow so you move with intention, not anxiety.

Make a plan that puts *you* in charge.

## Let Me Guess—You're Just Gonna Wing It?

Before you even open the conference app or browse the session schedule, stop and ask yourself: *Why am I going?* Not in the existential, "Why do conferences exist?" sense—but really, *what do you want to walk away with?*

Your answer will shape everything.

Most attorneys either go in hoping to meet "good contacts" or get some CLE credit. That's not a strategy. That's a default.

So let's get clear. What are your top three goals?

- ✓ Meet in-house counsel in your target industry.
- ✓ Reconnect with a few former colleagues or classmates who'll be attending.
- ✓ Raise your visibility—whether that's showing up on LinkedIn, getting noticed on a panel, or being seen with someone who's a connector.

Make it personal. Make it concrete. **And write it down.**

These goals become your filter for every decision you make about how to spend your time once you get there.

## Anchors Away

If you do nothing else—set up one or two anchor meetings before you arrive.

Anchor meetings are the planned moments that give *shape* to your day. Maybe it's coffee with a client, lunch with a connection, or a quick 15-minute walk-and-talk with someone you admire. It doesn't have to be big. It just has to be *on your calendar.*

Because when you have something locked in, your confidence shifts. You don't walk into a crowd thinking, *"Where do I even start?"* You walk in thinking, *"I already have a place to be."*

Use the conference app if there is one—this is where the tech finally works in your favor. You can usually search attendees, send short messages, and set up light-touch check-ins like:

*"I saw your panel and thought it was great—would love to hear more if you're free for a quick coffee during one of the breaks?"*

Sometimes that's all it takes to spark a conversation that goes deeper. Simple. Direct. Human.

The anchor meeting is your safety net. It's also your launchpad. One good connection early in the day can shift your whole energy.

And if they flake? You still showed up like someone with a plan.

Not everyone becomes a connection or client. And that's okay.

Chalk it up, laugh it off, and move on.

*Next!*

## Don't Wander. Map It.

You don't need a full-blown itinerary, but you do need a loose map—especially for the first few hours.

Why? Because the first hour sets the tone. If you start off aimless or hiding in the corner with your coffee, it's hard to shift that energy later.

Decide ahead of time:

- ✓ Where will you go first? (Registration, coffee area, session room?)
- ✓ Who might you see there?
- ✓ Is there someone you can meet or sit next to—someone already on your radar?

Even something as simple as saying, "I'm going to hit the first session early and sit near the front so I can ask a question," gives you purpose. It gives your body somewhere to go, and your mind something to focus on.

Make movement your default. Move through the space with lightness, curiosity, and direction. That doesn't mean you need to "work the room." It means you don't stall out. You keep your energy forward—even if it's just toward the coffee line.

Don't overthink it. Just don't wing it either.

## Pre-Screen Your People

Here's something most people never think to do: define the kind of person who's worth your time before you meet them.

This isn't about judging. It's about clarity.

You're not at the conference to talk to everyone. You're there to build traction with the *right* people. So set your own filters. Think about your best clients—the ones who get it, pay on time, and don't drain your soul. Who are they? What do they do? Now go find more of *them*.

This also helps you avoid wasting time on people who drain your energy. If you're clear on your value and your vibe, you'll spot a mismatch faster—and move on without guilt.

One more tip: look up the hotel ahead of time. Find out where the coffee shop is, where the bars and restaurants are, and where people naturally gather. You've now got the blueprint. You're not showing up hoping it all works out. You're walking in with strategy, intention, and a personalized plan. That's the difference between wandering a conference and *working* one.

Next, we'll talk about how to use that plan once you're in the room—how to move, how to listen, and how to leave an impression that lasts longer than a LinkedIn request.

# Chapter 7

# Small Talk Doesn't Mean Small Impact

You've done the prep. You've built the plan. You've landed at the hotel, picked up your badge, and scoped out where to grab a drink. You're in.

*Now what?*

You've made it past registration. You're in the hallway. Your lanyard is around your neck, your bag is slung, and now it's time to do the thing no one trains you for: strike up a conversation.

And for a lot of attorneys, that's the scariest part—because this is where it stops being about the law. You're not billing. You're not presenting. You're just… standing there, coffee in hand, trying to read the room without looking like you're scanning for the exit. No script. No safety net. Just you—ready or not.

Every hallway, panel break, and coffee station becomes a maze of unspoken expectations. No one hands you a roadmap. No outline. No back up. Just people standing around, hoping someone else makes the first move.

So you start spiraling:

- ✓ What do I say?
- ✓ How do I explain what I do?
- ✓ What if I say something awkward?
- ✓ What if I forget their name, or worse—mine?

This chapter is here to stop the spin. To help you speak like yourself—and be remembered for it.

Let me tell you what this looks like—because I just lived it.

I had just arrived at a conference where I only knew a couple of people, and I was totally new to the event. I was hungry, so I headed down to the hotel bar, grabbed a stool, and ordered a grilled cheese sandwich and tomato soup. Pretty ordinary, right? But that's the magic. That's where real conversations start—not in the ballroom, but at the bar with a grilled cheese and a soup of curiosity.

Rainmaker: Unleashed

Sitting next to me was someone else with a badge on. I turned and asked, "Are you here for the conference?" She said yes. I followed with, "Where did you fly in from?" Omaha, she said. And just like that—instant connection. I told her my parents live in Omaha, and that I grew up in Nebraska.

That simple moment turned into a real conversation. No name tags awkwardly stared at. No forced smiles. Just two humans bonding over soup, geography, and conference survival mode.

I wasn't working the room. I wasn't trying to make anything happen. I was just hungry—and willing to talk to the person next to me. And that's really all this is: being open enough to find the human thread. Because once you do? The rest is easy.

We're going to walk through exactly how to start conversations without sounding rehearsed, how to talk about your work without defaulting to your résumé, and how to recover when your brain decides to freeze mid-sentence.

Because rainmakers don't just speak—they connect. And once you get this part down? You'll walk into a room ready to connect with people.

## You Don't Have to Try That Hard

At the last conference I attended, these were my actual openers. Nothing polished, nothing rehearsed—just real-life, situational comments that opened the door. Forget the idea that you need a clever intro. You don't. You need something that feels natural and gets a genuine reaction. That's what makes people want to keep talking.

- ✓ "Have you gotten a headshot yet? I just got mine done and I'm hoping they turned out okay."
- ✓ "Is it just me or is it freezing in this hotel?"
- ✓ "What do you think of the conference so far?"

Use what's around you. The line for coffee. The session that just wrapped. Anything that gets a smile, a laugh, or even a knowing eye-roll is fair game.

This isn't about dazzling anyone—it's about cracking the silence just enough to make space for someone to respond. These aren't lines.

Rainmaker: Unleashed

They're just moments. Casual, human, and easy to build from. That's how I start conversations that actually go somewhere—without sounding rehearsed or making it weird.

You'll feel them start to relax—because what you're saying is just normal and ordinary. Not a pitch. Not a performance. Just human. That's the beauty of skipping the work talk. You disarm them. You make it personal without making it weird. And once they're relaxed, it's easy to say, "I'm Sejal. What's your name?" I don't jump from names to job titles.

That middle space? *That's where the real stuff happens.*

I ask where they're from, what made them come to this conference, if they're speaking.

We go back and forth—light, human, curious.

And then at some point, it happens.

The **infamous question**: *"So, what do you do?"*

Do you hear your inner voice kicking in, screaming 'Don't screw this up!'—and then, the mouth opens and the vomit begins.

Not because you mean to. But because in that split second, your brain flips to 'professional mode' and out comes a stream of credentials, titles, and industry buzzwords—like your brain went on auto pilot and got stuck. You can feel the energy shift. Their eyes glaze, their posture changes, and suddenly it's not a conversation—it's a power point in human form.

Here's what I want you to remember: ***You are not your résumé***. The assumption is basic—you're here at this conference, thereby you must have a brain.

You don't need to give a professional monologue. You need to talk like a real person who just happens to do excellent work.

Instead of: "I'm a partner of... (cue the zzzzs).

Me? I keep it short. I say, "I'm a non-practicing attorney." Then I flip it right back: "What about you—what do you do?" That's when the real work starts—not because I'm trying to come up with a perfect response, but because I'm analyzing them and flipping on my Emotional Quotient (EQ). I'm listening to what makes them tick—how they talk, what they value, and where the hook might be to build a real connection. I ask light questions that make them laugh: "Is this what 12-year-old you thought you'd be doing?" And I listen—really listen—to how they talk about their work, their role, and what matters to them. Only then do I craft the version of what I do that threads right into their world. That's not small talk. That's mental ninja-level rainmaking.

At one of my recent conferences, I had just stepped into a restroom stall when someone in the next one casually asked, "Are you presenting the workshop?"

I answered, "Yes!"—wondering how on earth she recognized me. But I rolled with it.

She said she was presenting the *other* workshop. Awesome. Mid-conference restroom bonding. Then she asked if I had any materials. I said no, still peeing. She said she'd send me hers. I said, "That's great!"—without ever seeing her face.

She left before I had any clue who she was.

The kicker: there was a third woman in the restroom too. Still in her stall. I laughed and said out loud, musingly, "I just had a whole conversation while peeing with someone I've never seen." She burst out laughing. We walked out of our stalls at the same time, still cracking up, and ended up having a real conversation after we left the restroom.

Was this strategic? Heck no. Did it build an unforgettable connection? Absolutely!

All while multitasking.

## Damn. I Just Forgot What I Was Saying.

We've all had it. The moment where your brain throws up a 404 error mid-sentence. You're talking. You're tracking. And then—Nothing.

Rainmaker: Unleashed

Your mouth is moving, but your mind just bailed.
And now you're standing there, eyes wide, wondering if you just blacked out or entered another dimension.

It's fine. Seriously. This happens to the smartest people I know. (Especially when we've been on back-to-back calls, three hours of sleep, and one sad protein bar.)

So what do you do when your brain bails mid-convo? You don't apologize. You don't spiral. You just own it: "Totally blanked on where I was going with that."

That's it.

Not sure how to say it in the moment? Use mine:

- ✓ "Wait—my brain just quit on me mid-sentence. What were we talking about?"

- ✓ "I swear I had a point. Man, it was good too."

- ✓ "Sorry—I just completely blanked. I think my brain left the room."

These work because they're real. They make people laugh. They defuse the moment. And more importantly—they make you relatable.

The secret: none of us are perfect. And when you say what everyone else is too scared to admit out loud? You make them feel safe.

That's the connection. That's the part they remember. Not that you blanked—but that you handled it like it was no big deal. You didn't screw up. You made it human.

## The People We Meet (and Wish We Didn't)

You'll meet all kinds of people at conferences—and some of them will make you want to fake a phone call just to escape. This isn't about judging anyone. It's about recognizing the energy in the room so you can respond strategically, not awkwardly.

Also? If one of these feels a little too familiar... yeah. That might be your cue to mix it up.

## The Talker

This one's easy to spot. They don't just talk—they perform. It's one long monologue about how important they are. They're telling you about their latest client win, the article they were quoted in, the keynotes they've done, and somewhere in there, maybe, you forgot why this conversation even started.

In your head, you're thinking: *"I get it. You're awesome. Sigh."*

Here's how you handle it.

Wait for a pause (or just cut in, softly but firmly). Then say, "That's impressive. I just realized—I haven't even introduced myself yet. I'm Sejal." And pivot hard: "What brings you to this conference?"

If they take the cue, great. If they bulldoze past it? You're done. Smile and say "So good chatting—I'm going to try to catch a few more folks before the next session. See you around."

No guilt. No weirdness. Just a smooth exit from a conversation that never included you in the first place.

## The One-Worder

Ever been in a conversation where you're doing all the work—and getting absolutely nothing back? You're smiling, you're trying, you're tossing out questions like lifelines... and getting answers that feel like you're interviewing a wall.

This is the person who answers every question like they're being deposed.

You: "Where are you based?"
Them: "Chicago."
You: "Is that where you're originally from?"
Them: "No."
You: "Oh, where are you originally from?"
Them: "St. Louis"
You: *(internally)* *"This is like pulling teeth."* Give me something!

They're not rude. They're not standoffish. They just have no conversational rhythm. Or maybe they hate small talk. Or maybe they just don't know how to get out of robot mode.

Rainmaker: Unleashed

Here's the move. They get one more chance.
Stop asking questions. Drop in a comment instead—something that doesn't need a response.

Like: "The gala had chicken I couldn't cut with a knife."

If they laugh or respond? You might crack them wide open…if not, oh well—that would not have been a fun working relationship. Give it a beat, then wrap: "Well hey, if I see you again later, I'll say hi."

You tried.

## The Speed-Dater
They clock your badge before they clock your face. Within seconds, they've asked what you do, scanned your lanyard, dropped their firm name, and casually mentioned the panel they're on. It's a hit-and-run interaction, and you can feel it.

They're already looking over your shoulder for someone more "valuable."

This isn't networking. You can feel it—this isn't about you.

You barely have time to say your name before they're handing you a card you didn't ask for and saying, "Great meeting you—let's connect!" And *poof*! They're gone.

What's wild: sometimes they don't even realize they're doing it. They think they're "maximizing" the event. But what they're really doing is leaving behind a trail of zero-connection conversations no one remembers.

If *you're* tempted to work a room like this? Stop. No one becomes a rainmaker by speed dating. They do it by making someone feel like the only person in the room.

The best conversations don't start with a pitch. They start with a laugh. A shared eye-roll. A grilled cheese sandwich. *Be human first. The rest comes easy.*

You traumatized?

Understandable.

*Next: let's find your kind of people.*

# Chapter 8

# Don't be a Wallflower

Let's be real: CLEs at conferences are like watching paint dry. No one's paying attention the whole time. People are checking their phones, thinking about lunch, or quietly slipping out to take a "call."

I ask a lot of my clients if they actually need CLEs for their licenses—because let's be honest, they can knock them out online while folding laundry. So why are they really sitting through these sessions?

The answer: it feels like doing something. It feels safe. Structured. Law school muscle memory.

But me? I'm not there for the credits. I'm at the coffee shop. I'm sitting in the couches. I'm wherever people are *actually* taking a break—because that's where the real conversations happen. That's where the people who are *also* done pretending to be glued to the panel end up. And that's my goal: to connect. Not to collect CLE credits.

Once you accept that most sessions are gap fillers—and maybe you'll hear something interesting, but probably not—then the real question becomes: what *should* you be doing instead?

So if you're ready to stop nodding through another panel you don't care about—let's dive in.

## Hiding in Plain Sight

Let's talk about why sessions feel so tempting—even when we know they're not the best use of time.

It's because they're safe. You don't have to introduce yourself. You don't have to make conversation. You just sit. Take notes. Nibble on a protein bar. Scroll Instagram under the table. And no one judges you.

It feels like "participating" without the awkward small talk. It lets you hide in plain sight.

But here's the catch: blending in doesn't build anything. It doesn't build relationships. It doesn't build a book. And it sure as hell doesn't build your reputation.

*Safety is a comfort zone, not a strategy.* And it's time to walk out of it.

## The Real Action? It's Not on the Agenda.

If you're skipping a session, skip it with purpose.

Because the good stuff? It's happening outside the breakout sessions. During the breaks. Near the latest cool gadgets at a vendor booth. On the couches near the bathrooms. That's where people go to take a breath—and that's your moment.

Your EQ muscle in action—real connection starts with knowing yourself really well. Me? I'm not a morning person—I'm a night owl. I know I won't be jumping into anything until the first break or lunchtime. And I'm an introvert, to the degree that I *need* to go back to my room for a mental reset. Not a nap—just a pause so I can be "on" when I need to be.

And when I am on? It's not working the room. It's sitting on a couch in the lobby. Someone I saw at the party last night sits down nearby. I drive the conversation: "I saw you at the party last night—what did you think?" Late night? No way I was making it to that panel. Just like that, we're talking. Not networking. Just two people catching their breath.

That's it. This isn't about being passive. It's about knowing where the real conversations happen—and showing up ready when they do.

Lobby bar, hotel lounge, conference couches—those are your opportunities. And remember back in Chapter 6 when we talked about walking in with a plan? This is where that prep pays off. You already scoped the hotel layout. You know where the high-traffic corners and low-key landing spots are. That wasn't just about logistics—it was strategy. These spots are where people stop performing and want a break. You're not interrupting anything. You're catching them in between—not at their most polished, but in the cracks where the real stuff lives. Don't force it. This isn't about walking up to random groups with your business cards. This is about picking up where real energy already exists.

*That's actually how I met Tiffany.*

*It was the first day of a conference—the welcome reception. I was thirsty, saw what looked like an opening in the bar line, and slid right in.*

Rainmaker: Unleashed

*Turns out? She was in line. I had just cut her.*

*I looked at her and said, "You snooze, you lose."*

*She laughed. We started talking. No pitch. No LinkedIn exchange. Just two people who dropped the pretense and connected.*

Tiffany has become a great friend.

That moment wasn't planned. It wasn't polished. But it was real. And real is what people remember.

## Stumbled? Good. Now You Know.

Some moments click. Others come out clunky. That's not failure—that's feedback.

Part of building your EQ is learning from *how* those moments feel. Were you being yourself, or slipping into perform mode? Did the conversation have energy, or did it fall flat?

*Good. Note it. Move on.*

Every "off" moment teaches you how to spot better ones. Every clunky exit makes the next one smoother. You're not here to be flawless. You're here to connect.

*Connection doesn't come from polish. It comes from presence.*

## No Regrets. Just Reps.

You're not going to nail every moment. That's ok.

You'll get tired. Misread the room. Blank mid-sentence.
That's okay. That's human. That's the work.

You'll talk to the wrong person too long—or blank right when the conversation finally gets good. That's ok.

This isn't about perfection. It's about building the muscle.

Rainmaking is practice. Creating muscle memory. Anywhere and Everywhere. You get better by doing it. Again and again. One moment at a time. One connection at a time.

I did it. So can you.

*Now that we've got you out of the sessions…*
*Let's make sure you don't burn out before the bar closes.*

# Chapter 9

# The Hidden Cost of Being 'On.'

*The night owl* — You can find me at the after party.

***It's intentional.*** I know when I'm having fun, people gravitate toward me. *That's when I'm magnetic.* That's when my energy is contagious. And here's the other thing: when I'm having fun, I attract the *right* people. ***Like attracts like.*** When I'm enjoying myself, I'm not pushing—I'm pulling. People who catch my vibe usually share my values—and those are the ones I actually want to work with. People loosen up after a drink—and I've learned that's when they open up faster, too. I stick to lighter drinks so I don't get brain fog. That lets me be sharp, present, and still have fun. ***It's not just social—it's strategic.*** Those first few minutes when everyone's guard drops? That's when real connection happens. The clients who become long-term, collaborative, easy partnerships? They didn't find me through a forced follow-up. They found me through shared energy—it wasn't forced.

It's not about working the room. It's about being the kind of person people want to talk to—the person who's clearly enjoying herself, not trying to close.

But that's *my* rhythm. That's what works for me. For you? It might be leaving the dinner early. Skipping the after-party. Maybe you're the one hitting the breakfast session. Maybe you vanish mid-day to walk, decompress, or recharge with room service and a spreadsheet. All valid. All rainmaker moves if they help you show up when it counts.

Your goal is not to power through every hour of a conference like it's a grind. ***Your goal is to manage your energy like the limited currency it is.*** Because if you burn it all in day one, you're not just tired—you're forgettable.

## Your Energy. Your Rules.

You don't have to match my pace. In fact, trying to copy someone else's rhythm is the fastest way to burn out—or worse, become invisible. The real win is figuring out *when* you naturally connect best and building your conference around that. You learned in the last chapter how to read the moment. This one's about reading *yourself.*

Rainmaker: Unleashed

*This is where self-awareness becomes your superpower. Be your own best friend—know what energizes you and protect it like hell.*

Self-awareness isn't just something you have—it's something you build by paying attention to your own patterns.

Are you sharper in the morning? Block that time for smaller meetings or more focused interactions. More of a slow-burn afternoon person? Save your key moments for the late-day energy lift. Hate cocktail hours but love a quiet breakfast? Great. Lean into that. Know when you need to be "on," and know when to disappear.

The power move isn't doing more—it's doing what works *for you*, with total clarity. **That's not flakiness. That's elite-level energy strategy.**

## Stay Sharp. Pivot Fast.

Even the best plan will need to flex. You might map out your ideal flow for the day—but then a conversation runs long, a session ends early, or your energy hits a wall.

Don't cling to the schedule. Adjust to the moment. This isn't about failing the plan—it's about being smart enough to shift when the energy does. You don't need to be perfect. *Perfectionism drains you.* And honestly—who wants the Stepford version of you? **Do you?** The goal isn't polished. It's present. Pivot when you need to. If the lobby energy is better than the panel? Stay. If your body's telling you to step away instead of shake more hands? Listen to it.

Rainmakers don't just know their rhythm—they know how to read the room and pivot. That adaptability is what keeps your presence strong without draining you dry. The goal isn't to execute your plan perfectly. The goal is to stay sharp, connected, and real—*even when the day doesn't go how you thought it would.*

You've already done the hard part: you showed up with intention. You mapped your energy—at least tried to. You practiced reading the room—maybe clumsily, maybe brilliantly, probably both. That's not perfection. That's progress. Now it's about staying present and letting even the messy moments build real momentum.

## The Underbelly of Conferences...

For the women out there, you and I know these situations. Often it boggles the mind that at a professional conference we're less protected—less guarded, less safe from commentary—than inside the firm. A gray area if you will.

You've felt it. And you know.

The weirdness.
The moments where the vibe shifts.
The comment that lingers.
The look that lasted too long.
The compliment that wasn't really a compliment.

You're standing there, trying to talk about litigation trends—and suddenly, someone's asking if you're married. Or if you've ever considered working in fashion. Or telling you they "never would've guessed you were a lawyer." Or just looked at you a bit too long?

Yeah. That's not professionalism. That's bullshit.

Welcome to the underbelly of conferences...

*Where you're expected to show up, speak smartly, smile politely...*

*...and where to pivot when someone comments on your body.*

*You weren't prepared for that. You shouldn't have to be.*

For me, I sometimes draw a blank. And inside? I'm furious. They don't just sting. They steal. These aren't just awkward moments. They're energy drainers. And no, it's not in your head. That pit in your stomach is data.

Because we've all learned to expect it. And prep for it. And pretend we're not.

- ✓ Do I call it out?

- ✓ Do I laugh it off?

- ✓ Do I risk being labeled "difficult" if I shut it down?

Rainmaker: Unleashed

- ✓ Do I leave the party early—and miss a real connection?

Sometimes, managing your energy isn't about introvert vs. extrovert. It's about power. It's about control. And it's about survival.

If you've ever walked out of a conference room and thought: *Why do I feel dirty?*

What do you do when they cross the line, and you're expected to smooth it over—so *they* don't feel uncomfortable?

## Boundaries Aren't Bad Behavior

You don't owe them comfort.
You don't owe them grace.
And you damn sure don't owe them your silence.

Some days, you'll freeze.
Some days, you'll clap back.
Some days, the smartest move will be to disappear.

You get to decide what's safe for you.
That's not retreat.
That's strategy.

**What the Hell Do You Do?**

When someone crosses the line—and you're the one expected to clean it up with a smile?

You're on the conference floor—not a courtroom. No HR. No recording. No referee. No witnesses. Just you, them, and a moment you didn't ask for.

The truth? You don't owe your ***composure***, your ***smile***, or your ***silence*** to anyone.

Not a judge. Not a GC. Not the guy who bought a round of drinks. Not the woman who pulls you aside to tell you your outfit is "bold." Not the managing partner who puts a hand on your lower back as he walks by.

**This is about power. And control.**

I know—I know. *"But my career…"*

So ask yourself: Is it worth it?

This is where strategy kicks in. Not because you're weak. But because you're brilliant—and smart enough to read the moment.

Some days, you'll confront it. With words. With silence. With a glance that says, *"Don't you dare."*

Other days, you'll walk away. Not because you're scared. Because you've got bigger plans than being their teachable moment.

None of those choices are wrong. They're just yours.

And that's the point: ***you get to choose.***

You don't have to play nice to play big. But you ***do*** have to protect your energy, your peace, your momentum.

Because your power isn't just in the comeback. It's in *the control*. Of how you move, how you *respond*, and *how you rise*.

## Small Shifts. Strategic Change.

There's a whisper of change starting to echo through this space.

I want to name one thing that gives me hope: there's an organization—quietly and powerfully—trying to make conferences safer for women. Operation Safe Spaces *(a task force founded by Women in eDiscovery)* is one of the first to offer real structure around accountability. It hasn't reached every event. But it's happening.

What used to be whispered between women in hallways is finally being said out loud. Conversations once kept private are becoming part of the keynote. The idea of safety is starting to be seen as a strategic priority—not an afterthought.

It's still early. But if you're reading this and wondering if you're the only one who feels this—you're not. You're not crazy. You're not dramatic. You're just awake. We're not just managing energy anymore. We're rewriting the terms.

Rainmaker: Unleashed

You've managed the room. Protected your energy. Reclaimed your power—even in the messiest moments. Now comes the part most people phone in… but not you.

The follow-up? That's not an afterthought. That's the conversion. The credibility. The difference between a one-off conversation and a long-term client.

*Let's talk about what happens when the name tag comes off—but the momentum doesn't.*

# Chapter 10

Rainmaker: Unleashed

# Still Thinking About That Great Conversation? *They're Not.*

You made it through the conference. Packed. Ready for Home.

Personally, I leave conferences on two notes: one, *man, I'm exhausted*, and two, *conference blues*. After nonstop motion, real connection, and all that energy, suddenly you're alone again. Swag in your suitcase. Faces in your head. That emotional dip? It's real. But here's the secret: how you follow up *right now* is what turns that high into something lasting.

You dodged the time-wasters, hit the moments that mattered, made real connections. Now comes the part where most people drop the ball: **the follow-up.**

And I don't mean a thank-you email or a "great to meet you" message sent from a plane while you're half-asleep. That's not follow-up. That's a formality.

This is where you turn a good moment into real momentum.

But not by jumping straight back into work mode. Your first message shouldn't be a pitch—it should feel like you picked up right where you left off.

Mine usually sounds like: "Hey, did you make it back okay?" or "You as wiped as I am?" Simple. Human. Real. Because here's the truth—it takes **7 to 8 interactions** to convert to revenue. You're not closing anything in the follow-up. You're keeping the connection warm so it has a shot at becoming something real.

If all things are equal—credentials, experience, polish—what makes someone want to work with you? Trust. Likability. That feeling of, *"You get it."* And you don't build that with one email. You build it by showing up—again and again. It's not about chasing. It's about being real. Be someone they'd actually want to talk to again. You know... be friends with your clients.

**Real rainmakers raise the bar—they filter out the fakes.**

## Did That Even Land?

I've walked out of conferences feeling like I killed it—and still caught myself wondering:
> Will anyone actually remember me?
> Or was I just another badge in the blur?

That's the thing no one talks about. The emotional hangover.
You give your energy. You show up. You connect. And then—
Silence.

That silence can make you question everything.
But that silence is also an opportunity.
Because most people disappear right here.
You? You follow up.
And that's the difference.

## Proof It Doesn't Have to Be Complicated

A few weeks ago, I was flying home from a conference. Still running on caffeine and adrenaline. And in that space where your brain's full—but the room is finally quiet.

So I pulled out my phone at the airport and started doing what most people forget to do: *I followed up.*

I sent LinkedIn invites—nothing fancy. Just quick messages:
*"Thank you for coming to my workshop."*
*"I appreciated your insights—I hope you'll reach out when you're in NYC."*

That's it.

*Not a pitch. Not a push. Just real. Thoughtful. Human.*

Guess what everyone's doing on the return day? Sitting at the airport, looking at their phones. Replies started coming in. Not because my message was perfect.

*Because I didn't let the moment die.*

Rainmaker: Unleashed

## Follow-Up Like a Friend

What makes follow-up easy? You weren't talking about work—you were talking about life. That's why it doesn't feel forced. It's just a continuation of the momentum you already built. That convo about your kids, your guilty pleasure TV show, or their favorite band? That's the stuff that makes a message feel like a friendship—not a pitch.

One message isn't the move. Real follow-up? It's a slow build—one thoughtful, casual check-in at a time.

You're *not* asking for a meeting. You're *not* circling back with a "just checking in." You *are* staying on their radar—without making it cringe.

- ✓ Share a podcast you talked about—travel, food, even reality TV.
- ✓ Send a callback to an inside joke or something quirky that came up.
- ✓ Add them on LinkedIn and write something personal, like "Still recovering from that panel lunch?"

Just keep it human. Don't force the tone or try to be funny unless you know the vibe is there.

These aren't *asks*. They're *reminders*. You're staying on their radar in a way that feels natural—so when they're ready, you're already the first name they think of.

Rainmakers don't follow up to chase work. They follow up—let's be honest—because there was a spark. It's not a pitch. It's rhythm. And when everyone else goes quiet, you're still showing up as you—and that's what they remember.

All that prep work—being intentional, setting up meetings, using the app, reading the room, knowing your rhythm—that's what got you here. None of it was just about the moment. It was about building a presence that sticks. Because now, in this quieter follow-up phase? This is when people decide if they want more of you.

**Real relationship = mutual investment.** You show up for them. Over time, they show up for you. That's not performance. That's *partnership*.

# The First Sign You'll Be Good to Work With

Follow-up isn't just a nicety. It's a test. And whether you know it or not, you're already taking it.

When someone hears from you after the conference, they're not just reading your message. They're feeling out how you move. Were you thoughtful? Did you listen? Did you actually remember what they told you in that hallway conversation?

That circling back is a preview. Of your style. Of your tone. Of what it would feel like to work with you when the stakes are real.

Because if your message is stiff, generic, or overly polished, they assume that's what working with you will feel like too. But if your message is clear, warm, and makes them smile—even just a little—they'll remember you because you cared.

You're not just following up. You're showing them what it feels like to be your client.

Don't overthink it. You already did the hard part—making the connection. Now it's just about showing up with the same energy, even when the room is quiet.
Keep the rhythm. Keep it real.

***That's how rainmakers stay remembered.***

And that's the thing no one tells you—what happens *after* the follow-up. What if they do respond? What if they say, "Yes, let's talk more."
Now what?

That's where most people freeze.
You got the door open… now you have to walk through it.
Let's talk about when you've got a captive audience and an actual hour?
Let's talk CLEs.

# Chapter 11

# CLEs Done Right = Clients in the Room

**You're not just giving a CLE. You're creating a client pipeline.**

*What's the actual purpose of presenting a CLE? Most of you think you're amazing presenters. You're not. And that's not just a problem—it's a missed opportunity.*

*So let's fix that.*

So what's the goal, really?

You show up. You read a script. You thank your co-panelists. You act like the audience is lucky just to hear you speak.

Then you read the slides. *Every. Single. Word.* Congratulations—you've just delivered the least effective hour of your year.

Do you want to be a law professor? Or worse—are you role-playing one?

*Stop.*

***So what's the real goal?*** A CLE isn't your moment to hear yourself talk and pat yourself on the back. It's your chance to be memorable—to *connect*, build *trust*, and turn *visibility* into actual conversations. Conversations that convert into clients.

You're not just presenting. **You're positioning.**

## The Real Reason CLEs Work

No one tells you: most of us were never taught how to present differently. We copy what we've seen. And what we've seen—especially in law—is slide decks, stiff scripts, and a race to sound impressive.

It's not your fault. But now you know.
*Be different. That's your responsibility.*

The real value of a CLE isn't in what you say—it's in how the room experiences you. It's in creating a moment that makes people want to

# Rainmaker: Unleashed

come talk to you afterward. That makes the follow-up feel personal, not *promotional*.

### You're Not Here to Lecture. You're Here to Land.

You're not a professor. You're not here to dump legal knowledge. You're here to translate it—make it stick, make it matter. When you present, your job is to make the room engage. *Think. Remember.*

That doesn't happen through slides. It happens through intention. Ask the audience a question that makes them pause. Give a hypothetical and challenge them. Tell a story they'll remember and repeat.

When you do that, you're not just teaching. You're creating a moment. And that moment builds connection.

*And connection? That's the front door to clients.*

## *Don't Waste the One Hour You Own*

Let's flip seats: what happens when *you're* the one at the front—presenting the CLE? *This is your hour. Your mic. Your room.*

Where else do you get a captive room of decision-makers, seated and listening—without distractions?

They're not walking out. They're not scrolling.
They're hearing *you*.

*That's when the audience hears you—it sinks in.*

So don't waste it trying to prove how smart you are.
Use it to connect. To spark curiosity.

Because when you use that hour well, it's not just CLE credit—it's the moment that makes someone walk up afterward and say: *"I want to talk to you."*

Rainmaker: Unleashed

## Design the CLE Like a Rainmaker

Anyone can teach a CLE. You're here to design one they *remember*. That means shaping the energy in the room—not just the slides on the screen.

Start with a quick story. Not your resume—something real. Something that earns attention and says, "This isn't going to be boring."

Tell them early: *"This is going to be interactive."* And mean it. Don't wait for the Q&A—build it in.

Add tension. Drop a laugh. Hit them with insight. You're not just teaching—you're pulling them in.

Every nod, question, or laugh is a crack in the wall. That's where trust starts. And trust is the conversion path.

You want them walking out thinking, *"I liked the way she framed that,"* not *"Wait... who was that speaker again?"*

## Make the Room Yours

CLEs are one of the few times you get a room full of professionals who are required to sit and listen. That's rare. Use it well.

Don't be afraid to say it: "I'd love to connect after this." Call out the common struggles in the room—the ones no one else is saying out loud. That's how you get the quiet nods. The *"She gets it"* energy.

Drop one detail they won't forget—a personal story, a sharp line, something sticky. If your CLE lands the right way, the talk doesn't end when the clock does—it starts working for you.

**The Hour Is Over. Now the Game Starts.**

A CLE without follow-up is a one-night stand. It's forgettable. A CLE with strategy behind it becomes your next referral source.

Reach out to the people who asked questions. Follow up with a resource tied to your presentation. Post a LinkedIn recap and tag the bar association, attendees, or co-presenters.

Rainmaker: Unleashed

Ask the organizer for an attendee list. Then send a quick "thanks for coming" email or add them on LinkedIn with a personal note.

You're not spamming—you're anchoring the moment.

*If you do nothing else,* send a personal message to three people in that room within 48 hours. It's the start of a rhythm—a rhythm that, done right, leads to clients.

One CLE done right can do what twenty *"let's catch up"* emails can't.

## The Room Was Yours. You Just Didn't See It.

My friend Rob—a partner at a major firm, chairs a practice group, and speaks constantly—once told me he thought CLEs were just a networking opportunity with his co-panelists.

He completely ignored the 60 people sitting in front of him, waiting to hear what he had to say. He thought he was there to impress the panel.

I told him: *"You're walking into a goldmine and waving politely as you leave."*

Once he shifted his focus to the audience—once he realized he was the authority in the room and every person there was a potential client—his entire strategy changed. And so did his pipeline.

CLEs aren't academic. **They're strategic.**

You've got a mic, a room of people who chose to be there, and an hour to make it count.

**Don't waste it being forgettable.** You don't need to be the smartest in the room. You need to be the one they *remember*. You made them listen.
Now let's make sure they don't forget you.

***A CLE is just one stage.***
But visibility doesn't stop when the mic gets clipped.

The same rule applies when it's your article in someone's inbox. Or your post on LinkedIn. Visibility isn't random—it's a constant.

*Be the one they remember.*

# Chapter 12

# Visibility Without Strategy Is Just Noise

If you're not writing, you're invisible. But let's write like a strategist—not a professor.

Are you the person who reposts your firm's updates without adding a word? Or the one who drops a law school case cite like it's a mic drop?

Be honest. If you weren't you, would you remember you?

*Presence isn't about proving you're smart.* It's about creating moments that make people want to work with you. Real presence is showing up where it matters—and showing up like a human, not a headline.

Most lawyers stay busy and call it strategy.

They say yes to panels that don't align with their work, post generic content that sounds like everyone else, and write articles no one reads—just to say they "put themselves out there." Some just repost firm updates without a single word of commentary and hope that counts as showing up.

**That's visibility wrapped in noise.**

Real visibility isn't about being seen everywhere.
It's about being remembered—in the right places.
A well-chosen panel. A sharp LinkedIn post. A story that hits because it's honest.

*Positioning* that lands is intentional, personal, and makes someone think, *"I want to talk to him."* Because when people remember how you made them feel, you're already halfway to a relationship.

To be clear: **being present isn't performative.**

Golf. My personal hell. I wasn't about to waste a perfectly good course full of clients just because I hate swinging a club. This is what it looks like to turn a bad fit into a power play.

I hate golf. Always have. It's just not my thing.

Rainmaker: Unleashed

Long story, but I was hosting a golf tournament—and I knew I had to show up. I wasn't about to swing a club, but I also wasn't going to waste the opportunity. I brought everyone there. Which meant I needed a way to network, connect, and be memorable—without pretending to love putting.

So I did what worked for me.

I grabbed Rich, jumped in a golf cart, and we drove hole to hole, taking group photos. At every stop, I got a moment with people. No awkward standing around. Just good energy, a little banter, and an easy excuse to follow up later.

After the tournament, I sent those photos out. Added a note. Something fun. Of course they knew where we met—duh, photo. You'd be shocked at how many responded. I wasn't just a name anymore—I was a memory. A conversation. A relationship, already in motion.

That's visibility done right. Not the loudest. Just the most intentional.

Done right, people see you authentically. It's not about doing what everyone else does. It's about showing up in a way that makes people want to keep talking to you. You don't need to sound brilliant on stage or publish the perfect article. You need to show up with clarity, connection, and a point of view.

The goal isn't applause—it's **alignment**.

A five-minute comment in the *right* room can do more than an entire keynote in the *wrong* one.

One LinkedIn post with a real opinion beats a dozen ghostwritten articles.

Visibility that works doesn't require volume. It requires voice.

One post doesn't make you visible. One article doesn't make you a thought leader. Visibility is earned through repetition—*strategic* repetition. Say something worth remembering, then say it again in a new way next month. That's how reputations are built. Not from volume—but from frequency + clarity.

# Forget the Checklist. What Actually Lands?

So, you're ready to show up. But here's the thing—*there's no one-size-fits-all way to get noticed*. Speaking, writing, social media—they all do different things. The key is knowing what each one *actually* does, so you're using it with intention—not just checking a box.

***Think of it like a conversation starter.***
Each format gives you a different way in—so pick the one that actually sounds like *you*.

- ✓ **Speaking** puts you in the room.

- ✓ **Writing** puts you in their head.

- ✓ **Social** puts you in their feed.

Each one gives you a different opening—but the goal is the same: create a connection that doesn't feel transactional.

*Speaking is the fastest way to make people feel you. See you. React to you.*

It's not about delivering a perfect presentation. It's about being the one they remember. That rarely comes from slides—it comes from truth. A story. That one line everyone's thinking but no one else has the guts to say.

*Writing is where you show how you think.*

But most legal writing? *Sterile, safe, forgettable.* If your article could've been written by anyone else at your firm, it's not helping you stand out—it's just filling space.

Strong writing should sound like *you*. It should spark a reaction, not just prove you know the law.

Speaking, writing, and posting all have the same job: *to get someone to engage with you.*

Not clap. Not reshare. *Engage.* That means they comment. They message you. They bring it up in a meeting. They feel like they know you well enough to start a conversation.

*That's the moment visibility becomes rainmaking.*

*Gut check:* Before you post or speak, ask yourself—will someone feel something? A laugh, a nod, a pause, a "damn, that's true." If not, it's not visibility—it's noise. Rewrite it. Sharpen it. Make it land.

## What You Think Works—Doesn't

At first glance, it looks like you're doing all the right things. You're out there. But just because you're active doesn't mean you're effective. If no one's remembering you, you're not being remembered—you're just busy.

You want to know what kills relevancy faster than anything?

- ✓ Posting a white paper with zero commentary, like we're all just dying to read 12 pages of citations.

- ✓ Reposting your firm's award announcement without saying *why* it matters—or why we should care.

- ✓ Writing a thought leadership piece so buttoned-up it sounds like it was ghostwritten by a junior associate trying not to get fired.

No one hires someone they can't *feel.* And if your writing reads like a compliance memo—or your social posts sound like you're scared of saying something wrong—you're not visible.
You're *forgettable.*

If you want real traction, stop performing and start connecting. Share something you believe. Tell a story that shows your point of view. Speak like you're having a conversation—not giving a keynote.

You're not building a following. You're building familiarity. And that's what opens doors.

Visibility doesn't make you credible.
**Presence makes you known.**

And being known isn't about racking up likes or having the flashiest LinkedIn banner. It's when someone says your name in a pitch meeting. When a GC tells a colleague, "You should talk to her—I keep seeing her name." That's presence. That's reputation. And that's what opens doors.

And once you're known, everything gets easier—because you're no longer invisible. You're already in the room. Now they're listening.

*So say something worth remembering.*

## Visibility Isn't the Goal. It's the Door.

Getting noticed isn't enough. The real power move is knowing what to do *after* they notice you. When someone messages you after your post, when a GC lingers after your panel, when a colleague says "that thing you wrote really stuck with me"—That's your opening.

Visibility opens the door.

*The next move is what gets you hired. And that's exactly what we're covering next.*

# Chapter 13

# Rainmaking Isn't Earned—It's Claimed

You're waiting for a sign. A signal. Some magical moment where you feel ready—experienced enough, credentialed enough, worthy enough—to start asking for the work.

*That moment doesn't exist.*

You don't earn your way into rainmaking. You claim it—by speaking up, showing up, and shutting down the mental gymnastics that say you're not ready yet.

What's the reason you haven't reached out? Followed up? Or asked for the damn meeting? It isn't because you don't know how. It's because you still think rainmaking means becoming someone you're not.

You've got that voice in your head whispering: "I'm not ready. I don't have enough experience. I need more credentials. I don't want to sound pushy." Sound familiar?

Or maybe you've convinced yourself that if you just keep doing good work, someone will eventually notice—because "my work speaks for itself," right?

**Spoiler: it doesn't. Not in the way you need.**

Meanwhile, Smooth-Talking Chuck is out here at the networking event saying, "I'll do whatever it takes to get work from you," like he's auditioning for a sad reality show called *Desperation: Esq.* And yet somehow, Chuck still thinks he's winning. He delivers that cringey one-liner, flashes a half-smile, and walks away like he just closed a deal.

Meanwhile, everyone in the room is silently praying he doesn't circle back. No one buys from him. They just remember how uncomfortable he made them feel—and how fast they'd say no if he ever followed up.

Let's stop pretending the work goes to the best attorney. Let's stop pretending you'll magically feel "ready" once you've done enough. Let's stop acting like the people landing the clients are the smartest or most experienced—they're not. They're just the ones who stopped waiting.

Rainmaker: Unleashed

*You in?*

## Expertise Isn't Enough

You've been told your whole life that hard work gets you noticed. But law is full of brilliant people who are invisible—because no one ever taught them how to matter to the client. Not by being loud. Not by being flashy. Just relevant.

The kind of person clients think of—without hesitation.
You get remembered because you matter—to *them*.

It's not about being everywhere. It's about being real.
You're not auditioning. You're building trust.
Not once. Not when you need something. Over time.

*Consistency is the difference.*

It's remembering a conference chat—and following up. "Can't believe it's been six months—what have you been up to?" when there's nothing in it for you. It's making a connection that has nothing to do with legal work—but everything to do with how they see you.

That's how people start to remember you.
That's how real relationships start to grow.

That's what rainmaking really is:
Slow momentum that suddenly looks like luck to everyone else.

## It Starts as a Strategy. Then It Becomes Natural.

At first, it's going to feel like extra effort. Like one more thing squeezed between billing hours and client emails. But if you do it right, it won't stay that way.

What starts as strategy becomes instinct. The check-in. The follow-up. The "just thinking of you" note. It stops being a task—and becomes second nature. Not because you're trying to get something. But because that's who rainmakers are: *they stay connected.*

You don't have to become someone else to do this well. No faking extroversion. No draining events. No forced small talk. And definitely no posting every week just to stay visible.

You just need to be intentional.

Rainmaking doesn't reward the loudest voice.

It rewards the one who *listens*, *remembers*, and *shows* up when it counts.

When you show up like that—clear, consistent, and low-pressure—people start to trust you. Not because you impressed them. Because you remembered something that mattered. Because you didn't just reach out when you needed something.

Because your presence isn't a pitch. It's a pattern.

That's how trust gets built. That's how the "let's keep in touch" actually turns into a client. You only need a few people who trust you—because you showed up when it mattered. That's what earns the call. That's what gets you invited in.

*Not volume. Not performance. Just intention, repeated.*

Let me give you another example—outside the law.

My sister-in-law Amy is the Chief of Staff at a logistics company. Her job isn't just logistics and ops—it's trust. She works across the entire business, with teams who move fast and decisions that carry weight. And she's the person everyone turns to—not because she's the loudest, but because she's the one they trust to get it right.

She knows what's happening before it happens. She picks up on tension before it explodes. She remembers the details that make people feel seen, and she follows through so consistently, people never have to chase her.

She doesn't need a spotlight. She already has influence.
And that's the difference.

What makes Amy good at her job isn't just execution. It's presence. Pattern. Intention. Relationships. The exact same things that make a great rainmaker.

## Start Where You Actually Are

Stop worrying about what you haven't done. The clients you didn't follow up with. The conferences you coasted through. The conversations you let fizzle out.

You didn't mess it up. You just didn't know what to do—*yet*.

*And now you do.*

Start with one person. Not your dream client. Not someone you barely know. Someone you already like. Someone you'd actually enjoy grabbing coffee with.

*No pitch. No preamble. Just connection.*

Because the fastest way to build rainmaking momentum isn't through strategy—it's through motion.

*And motion starts with people who make it easy to show up.*

You've already read my story. Indian woman from Nebraska. No pedigree. No built-in network. And still—I figured it out. Not because someone opened the door for me. But because I stopped trying to prove I belonged and started acting like I did.

**Authentically.**

## Flatten the Curve: Make It a Line, Not a Wave

Most attorneys live in a cycle. When billables are high, they don't have time to think about getting clients. When billables are low, they panic—and suddenly it's all coffee meetings, LinkedIn posts, and "let's catch up" emails. The graph spikes and crashes. I've seen it a hundred times.

My job? Flatten the wave into a line.

So you're not scrambling for work one quarter and drowning in it the next. So your outreach isn't reactive—it's *consistent*. So when a need comes up, they think of you—not because you chased them, but because you showed up smart.

Smart showing up doesn't mean doing the most. It means doing the right thing, at the right time, for the right reason. It's the check-in that isn't random. It's the article that actually lands. It's the intro that makes sense—not one that feels forced.

This isn't about being everywhere. It's about being strategic. The goal isn't exposure for the sake of exposure—it's relevance that actually lands. Over and over. The biggest threat to momentum isn't talent. It's inconsistency.

*And the excuse is always the same: "I've just been slammed lately."*

We both know what that means. You got busy. You stopped reaching out. You told yourself you'd pick it up later—but "later" became three months, then six.

Now it feels awkward to re-engage. So you avoid it.

Momentum dies. Guilt takes over. And that's how smart attorneys start over again and again—never realizing how much credibility they're losing every time they disappear.

## Do This Instead.

You don't apologize. You don't over-explain. You don't pretend the gap didn't happen. You just restart.

You pick one person. You say something that matters. You move forward.

That's it. No guilt. No drama. Just motion.

Because the longer you wait, the heavier it feels. And momentum doesn't come from overthinking—it comes from one clean move.

## Build a Rhythm You'll Actually Keep

This isn't about building a system that looks good on paper. It's about building one you'll actually use. Rainmaking only works if it fits your real life. Not someone else's version. Not your firm's idea of what outreach "should" look like.

Rainmaker: Unleashed

If you're an introvert—great. If you hate small talk—same. If you don't want to post on LinkedIn every week—don't. What matters is that you stay in motion in a way that feels like you—and works when things get busy.

Maybe that means sending one thoughtful email a week. Or checking in with five contacts a month. Or following up with anyone you connected with at a conference—within five days, no matter what.

*It doesn't need to be fancy. It needs to be consistent.*

Because a rhythm isn't about doing more. It's about doing enough—over and over again—until people start to associate you with connection, not performance.

That's what transforms you from a commodity into a trusted advisor. Not your résumé. Not your law school. Your rhythm. And when the momentum slips? Because it will—just get back in it.

There's no penalty box. No client is keeping score. *It's a soft skill. A rhythm.* Like working out, or writing, or actually learning how to listen.

You don't lose it when you miss a week. You just lose momentum when you convince yourself it's too late to start again. The real goal isn't to get it perfect. It's to keep it moving. Because rhythm builds relationships. And relationships build everything else.

Let's be clear—this isn't about habits for habit's sake. We're here for revenue. Consistent, compounding revenue.

A real rhythm doesn't just get you noticed. It makes you predictable—in the good way. It means you've got a pipeline, not a panic spiral. It's what keeps you from one quarter of "crushing it" to the next where no one remembers your name.

## What does this all mean?

You've built *momentum. Consistency. Revenue.*

Now stop waiting. Do it.

Rainmaker: Unleashed

Look—if you're fine being an average lawyer, great. Keep doing what you're doing. Coast. Get staffed. Hope someone throws you work. But if your goal is to be a practice leader—if you want your own fiefdom, your own crew of associates, your own stream of clients—then this is what it takes.

This is how you get off the bench and into control. No more scrambling. No more waiting.

**Power isn't handed to you. You build it.**

You've done enough waiting.

It's time to start choosing where your energy goes—and who actually deserves it. Because not everyone is your client. And that's not a weakness.

*That's your edge.*

You ever wonder why some attorneys have books of business that follow them from firm to firm? It's not because they're the loudest. Or the most credentialed. It's because the relationship is that deep.

*The trust is that strong.*

At some point, the firm name stops mattering. Because the client isn't staying for the firm—they're staying for the person.

They didn't hire the brand.

They hired *you*.

## When I Realized I Didn't Need Backup

Early on, I brought a junior partner with me to a client meeting. I had set it up. I had *the* relationship. I just thought it would be good to have someone with subject-matter expertise in the room.

Big mistake.

We sit down. Client's barely had a sip of coffee. And this guy—without warning—leans forward, *bangs on their desk*, and says:

Rainmaker: Unleashed

**"What's it going to take to win work? I'll leverage rates. What do you need?"**

I wanted to slide under the table.
The client froze. I recovered what I could, but the damage was done.
And from that day on? I never took him to another meeting.

Fast forward a few months—I'd secured a major opportunity. Decision-makers from across a company were flying in globally for one meeting. High-stakes. High-visibility. I asked internally if there was anyone with expertise who could come with me.

And guess who the firm recommended?

Yep. Desk-banger.

I said no. I told them he was too green to meet those leaders. I didn't trust him. I wasn't going to risk my relationships on someone who couldn't read a room.

I cancelled the meeting.

Let me say that again:
*I walked away from a high-stakes, high-visibility opportunity—because I knew that showing up with the wrong person could cost me everything I'd built.*

Firm leadership was furious.
They were stunned I pulled the plug.
But I didn't flinch. I knew I made the right call.

Because I'd already learned what happens when you trust someone's bravado over your own gut. *Confidence doesn't equal client-ready.* And I wasn't about to hand off relationships I'd built just to play nice internally.

Luckily, at the time, I had a boss who backed me—Randy handled the fallout.

And that moment taught me both truths at once:
*Protecting the relationship is your job. But having someone behind you when you do? That matters too.*

That was the day I stopped asking if I could lead.
**I just did.**

You've built the momentum. You've shown up with intention. Now it's time to get selective. Because not everyone deserves your energy.

**Not everyone needs to be a client.**

# Chapter 14

# Not Everyone Needs to Be a Client

***Quality over quantity.*** Why are you chasing everyone—even the ones you don't even like?

You're not doing charity work. You're building a business. And the people who actually resonate with you? They make better clients. They tell you what's wrong on an engagement. They pay their bills on time. And guess what? You actually enjoy working with them.

It's efficient. It's collaborative. Sometimes—it's even *fun*.

You can't build a powerful book by trying to win over everyone. Just because someone has a big title—or a sexy company name—doesn't mean they're your person. If the energy's off or the values don't align? Every interaction becomes a grind. And sooner or later, you're not just drained. You're stuck in uncomfortable positions on cases you never should've taken.

Chasing the wrong people doesn't build momentum. It builds resentment.

You don't need to explain why someone isn't a fit. You just need to recognize it early—and move. That's not harsh. ***That's rainmaker instinct.*** Because the longer you try to force chemistry, the more you lose your edge.

This is your time. Your energy. Your name. *Protect it like it matters—because it does.*

You're not here to prove you're likable. You're here to build something that lasts.

***Does everyone need to like you? Seriously—who cares?*** Rainmakers don't chase everyone. They filter early—so they can show up fully for the right ones.

You know that client who makes you fake laugh on Zoom? Or the one you physically groan at when you see them walking up at a bar event? Yeah. That's not a client. That's a warning sign.

Rainmaker: Unleashed

If you wouldn't want to grab a drink, join a nonprofit board, or sit on a panel together—why are you trying to work with them?

***If it's a no… then what are you doing?***

And tell me this—when did we start pretending that liking someone was optional? You're spending hours with this person. Your brainpower. Your name on the line. *Likeability matters.*

Shared values aren't nice-to-haves. They're the shortcut to trust. When you care about the same things—a cause, a community, a way of operating—the relationship flows faster. You don't have to over-explain your tone, your fees, or your boundaries. They just get it.

When it clicks, everything gets easier. You follow up faster. You speak more freely. You want to show up. And when it doesn't? You drag your feet, dodge their emails, and secretly hope they disappear. That's not a client relationship. That's emotional debt.

Some clients don't demand more work. They demand more of *you.* They want the constant handholding. The instant response. The ego massage. The endless "quick calls" that aren't quick. And somewhere along the way, you stop doing your best work—because you're too busy managing *them.*

A partner I went to law school with—smart, senior, no-nonsense—spent an entire weekend trying to deliver on a client request that never had clear guardrails.

The client never discussed budget. That was the first problem.

Then came the shifting expectations. What they originally asked for got redefined halfway through. The timeline changed. The requirements expanded. And there was no clear deliverable in sight.

The partner kept adapting—expecting it to stabilize. And they delivered. But by Monday, the client ended up receiving a substantial discount. Not because the work wasn't done. But because the scope was blurry, the expectations kept shifting, and no one stopped to define success upfront.

Just a wasted weekend that could've been spent watching Netflix instead of spiraling in ambiguity.

It looks like service. But it chips away at your time, your value, and your sanity. That's erosion.

And the worst part? This wasn't someone new to client work. This was a rainmaker. Someone who *knows* how to manage complexity. But when engagements start without alignment, even the most experienced attorneys can end up shouldering confusion that gets mistaken for inefficiency.

They don't just drain you. You end up doing your worst work—not because you aren't capable, but because you're too busy managing them. They stall your momentum. Block better clients from your calendar. Slow down decisions. Complicate outcomes. Suck time into their drama and indecision. And then they have the nerve to haggle your invoice.

Let's be honest—we've all had them.

Let's call it what it is: ***Bad clients are emotional abusers.*** They ignore boundaries. Question your judgment. Make everything feel like your fault.

And the worst part? You start second-guessing yourself—like *you're* the problem for being overwhelmed. You're not. You're just under siege by someone who should've never made it past your filter.

***The poison:*** Zero referrals. Every time you talk to them, they just want to bitch. And when they finally do mention your name? Now they're bitching about *you*. Of course it's not about your work. It's because you didn't bend to their chaos.

This isn't about being sensitive. It's about being strategic. Because when you're constantly managing the person—not the work—everything slows down. You lose time, clarity, and the spark that makes you sharp.

*Rainmakers don't operate under emotional duress. They operate in flow.*

**This is why filtering isn't rude. It's how you protect your revenue—and your damn time.**

You get to choose too. You're not the one trying to get picked. You're not auditioning. You're assessing. The best rainmakers don't walk into

### Rainmaker: Unleashed

meetings hoping to be chosen. They walk in asking: *"Is this someone I even want to work with?"*

## Why that mindset matters?

*Years ago, I set up a meeting with a senior partner—a relationship I was hoping to build. I brought a male colleague with me, thinking we'd show up as a team.*

*We walk into the conference room. The partner is already seated, waiting.*

*And my colleague—without thinking—turns and hands me his coat.*

*I was so stunned, I just stood there. Holding it. In front of the partner. In a room I had arranged. In a meeting I had planned.*

*And just like that, I wasn't the lead. I wasn't even a peer.*

*The tone shifted instantly. I couldn't recover from it. That relationship never developed. And honestly? I don't even blame the partner.*

*I looked like someone's assistant—because that's how I was treated.*

*That was early in my career. I didn't know how to protect my own presence yet. But after that?*

*I never let it happen again.*

*My rule:* Don't bring anyone into a room until you've earned the relationship yourself. They need to know who you are. They need to see your value. Otherwise, all it takes is one stupid moment—and you're invisible.

When you forget that? You take on anyone who shows interest. You twist yourself to fit their expectations. You convince yourself it's "just for now." And suddenly, you're knee-deep in a mess you never wanted—underpaid, undervalued, and wondering how you got stuck.

**Why?** Because this is your career. Your reputation. Your name on the invoice. If someone doesn't respect that from the start? They don't get a second conversation.

When you're consistently building real relationships?

You get to pick. You *should* be picky. **You earned that right.**

## Red Flags That Look Like Green Lights

You already know what the drainers feel like. This is what they sound like at the start. They don't come in loud. They come in casual. *Vague. Slippery. Collaborative.*

Watch for lines like these:

- ✓ "I just need a quick favor…"
- ✓ "Let's hop on a call and talk through options."
- ✓ "We're not ready to hire yet, but want your perspective."
- ✓ "Can you just look this over and tell me what you think?"
- ✓ "I have a few ideas I'd love to bounce off you."
- ✓ "We'll figure out the budget later."

***Translation:*** No direction. No commitment. No respect for your time.

And if you're still unsure?

*Ask yourself this:*
*Is this relationship moving forward—or just circling my energy?*

## Alignment Isn't Fluff. It's Your Filter.

Let's be clear—alignment isn't a vibe. It's not just surface-level chemistry—like liking the same TV shows or ordering the same drink at the bar. It's about how someone moves. How they make decisions. How they treat people when they're stressed. When that aligns with how *you* operate? Everything moves faster. Trust builds quicker. And the work gets easier—*because you're not spending energy constantly translating, explaining, or adjusting.*

Rainmaker: Unleashed

When alignment is missing, you feel it immediately. You start hedging. Softening your tone. Playing small to keep the peace. And every time you second-guess yourself, you chip away at your own confidence. Not because you're unsure—*but because the client doesn't get you.*

That doesn't make them a bad person. It just makes them *not your client.* Fit isn't about being agreeable. It's about being aligned. And the more honest you are about who you work best with, the faster the right clients will find you—and the easier it'll be to deliver real results.

*This goes back to what we talked about earlier: self-awareness.*
The better you know yourself, the easier this gets. Because once you're clear on how *you* work, you can be honest with yourself about who you work best with.

**Protect Your Peace.**

You've heard it in psychology: if you want something new to enter your life, you have to make space for it. The same applies here. When you're cluttered with bad fits, draining clients, or people who don't respect your time—you leave no room for the ones who do.

This is your bandwidth. Your business. Your name on every deadline and every deliverable. You don't owe your time to anyone who chips away at your clarity. **Protect your peace. Because your time isn't free— and neither are you.** When the client fits, everything flows—your fees, your follow-up, your future.

*You've done the filtering.*

Now let's talk about what happens when you stop trying to look the part—and actually start playing your game.

# Chapter 15

Rainmaker: Unleashed

# Apparently I Missed the Memo on Golf and Scotch

*I once threw a Diwali party—not just for clients, but judges, AUSAs, and in-house counsel. Why? Because everyone loves a room full of smart, interesting people.*

*I wasn't just hosting. I was aligning puzzle pieces.*

*This wasn't a firm-hosted event. It was my thing. An Indian restaurant in NYC—sarees, samosas, candles everywhere, Bollywood music playing. No spouses. Just real connection.*

They got a piece of me and my story.

They got to know the *real* me.

They stayed. And not one of them left thinking it was unprofessional.

In fact, I got more follow-ups, more "Hey, I want to talk to you about something," more traction from that one night than from any networking dinner with three forks and a wine pairing. It wasn't just fun—it was intimate. It created closeness. Because I opened the door to my culture, they walked through—and they remembered how it made them *feel*.

That party wasn't strategic.

It was personal.

It was mine.

And it worked.

*One of my clients—sharp, funny, and finally seeing rainmaking through a new lens—decided to do the same. He threw a backyard cookout with ribs, cornbread, a DJ spinning old-school R&B, and dominoes clacking in the corner.*

*And his clients? They loved it.*
*Not because it was buttoned up—but because it wasn't.*
*Because they got to see him.*

*Not the résumé. Just unfiltered him. Because when you stop trying to fit the mold—and start moving how you actually move—people feel it. You become memorable without even trying.*

Law firms won't always say it, but there's still an unspoken mold of what a "real rainmaker" looks like: extroverted, golf-loving, scotch-sipping. If you don't match it, the silence is loud—and it's easy to start thinking you're the one doing it wrong.

**Here's what no one tells you: you don't have to play it that way.**

And if you've spent your career feeling like you're five degrees off the default—you're not behind. You're just finally in the right chapter.

## Be Yourself

The biggest myth in rainmaking? That there's only one right way to show up. That if you just look polished enough, act like you belong, and mirror the firm's top partner—you'll get invited in.

Heck, I've been written up for having "too sexy" hair. Apparently, long hair was offending folks.

But let's be honest—most attorneys are still playing dress-up. They're performing professionalism instead of owning presence. They say what they think they're supposed to say. Mirror the people they think matter most. And underneath it all, they're exhausted. *Burnt out.*

Why doesn't it work? Because people can *feel* the disconnect.

If you've ever walked into a room and felt like you had to become someone else just to be taken seriously—you know exactly what I'm talking about.

You're not building credibility. You're auditioning. And the problem with auditions? You're always waiting to get picked.

## What Actually Builds Confidence

At a recent conference, a woman came up to me after my session and said, "I wish I had your confidence." I smiled.

Rainmaker: Unleashed

"This isn't confidence," I told her.
***"It's finally knowing my worth."***

That's what confidence actually is—not pretending to know everything, but knowing your lane so well that nothing shakes you.

Confidence isn't a power suit. You can't fake it. It's something you *build*—by getting honest about what you're good at, how you move, and what rooms actually bring out your best. Once you know that, you stop performing. You stop auditioning. ***And you start leading.***

Confidence doesn't come from credentials. If it did, every attorney with a top-tier résumé would feel bulletproof—and we both know that's not true. *Real confidence comes from alignment.* From doing the things you're naturally good at, in ways that actually feel good to you.

That's where the energy shows up. That's when people start saying, *"There's something about her..."*

One of my favorite client moments? I invited a group to a Depeche Mode concert. I told them to ditch the suits at the office and show up in their favorite '90s band T-shirts. And they *did*. We danced, we screamed lyrics, we laughed all night. No pitch. No pressure. Just energy.

What happened? The feedback? Those clients felt closer to me in one night of being real than they ever had at years of formal dinners. That's confidence—not because I stood out, but because I stopped trying to blend in.

That night wasn't a deviation from rainmaking. ***That was rainmaking in action.*** I wasn't dragging them into my strategy—I was inviting them into my world.

When you stop trying to mimic someone else's client dinners, calendars, or coffee schedule, everything shifts. Your rhythm becomes the strategy. Whether you're a slow-burn relationship builder or a burst-of-energy connector—own it. When you lean into how you actually move, that's when things start to click. And clients feel it.

My secret: invite *everyone*. Even if they say they can't come, you've still created a touchpoint. You've still shown them a piece of who you are. ***Bring the FUN—not boring.*** Now you've got a reason to follow up— grab lunch, set up coffee, talk about the concert. That's rainmaking disguised as an invite. You're not just filling seats. You're building connection.

## Your Background Isn't a Barrier. It's Your Strategy

Let's get something straight: if you've ever been told to tone it down, play it safe, or stop drawing attention to yourself…that wasn't strategy. That was fear disguised as advice. **My advice: Stop Listening.**

Some of us weren't raised to self-promote. We were raised to work hard, stay humble, and hope someone noticed. We were taught to be grateful for a seat—not to ask who built the damn table. *I create bigger tables.*

*The thing is: when you grow up outside the system, you don't just learn how to survive.*

You learn how to translate.
How to read a room fast.
How to speak ten different professional dialects.

That's a strength.
That's leverage.
**Use it.**

You don't build trust by blasting credentials. You build it by meeting people where they are—and that's something outsiders do instinctively. When you've had to adapt your entire life, you know how to read the unsaid. You catch the pauses. The tells. The subtext.

**That's not just emotional intelligence—it's rainmaker intelligence.** Because clients don't just want expertise. *They want to feel understood.*

## Quiet Doesn't Mean Forgettable

There's this idea that to be good at rainmaking, you have to be the most outgoing person at the event. The one holding court at the happy hour. The one who works the crowd like they're running for office.

*That's not strategy. That's theater.*

Real strategy is knowing your strength—sitting in it.

If you're the one who picks up on what's *not* being said, sends a sharp follow-up email, or remembers someone's daughter was sick last week? That's presence. That's power. You don't need to steal the spotlight. You just need to leave an impression.

What I tell my clients: your only job at a cocktail party is to make two new friends. That's it. You're not there to impress the whole room. You're not getting hired after one interaction. So take the pressure off. Go find two interesting people. Be real. Be curious. And then go home. That's rainmaking too.

## This Is Where You Build Your Playbook

You've spent most of your career trying to fit into someone else's blueprint. Throw it out. Trying to walk in someone else's shoes gives you blisters. And maybe that got you this far—*limping*. Does it take you where you want to go?

This is the moment to stop mimicking and start designing.
***Look inward. Let that be your guide.***

Now that you know how you're wired—your pace, your energy, your strengths—you can build a strategy that actually fits you. One that feels natural. **Repeatable. Powerful. Yours.**

You're on the path to building your playbook, so we need to talk about something that kills more rainmaking than lack of skill ever could: *how you spend your time.*

*Because you don't need more hours in the day. You need to stop wasting the ones you already have.*

# Chapter 16

# So Busy. When Do I Do This?

You've got 17 deadlines, 143 unread emails, and court. Cool. Let's talk.

You're already behind on work. Your inbox is a war zone. You've got client fires, internal politics, and at least one partner who thinks "quick call" means 45 minutes. And now I'm over here telling you to block time for rainmaking? Yeah—I get it. It feels impossible.

*This Isn't About Time. It's About Attention.*

But let's be honest—this isn't really about bandwidth.
It's about attention.

And if you don't start protecting even a sliver of it for your future? You're going to spend your whole career reacting to someone else's priorities.

Again, it just depends on what you see in your future.

## Where Your Time Actually Goes

You don't need eight hours of free time to make rain. You just need to stop giving away the sharpest part of your day to nonsense. The endless re-editing. The calls that could've been emails. The fake urgencies. You say yes because it feels faster—but every yes is a withdrawal from the time you *said* you didn't have. And before you know it, the day's gone. Not because you weren't working. But because you never got to *your* work.

## You Make Time for What You Care About

The part no one wants to admit: you make time for the people you actually care about. Your kids. Your friends. Your family. Even your favorite coworker who needs to vent. The problem isn't time—it's how you mentally categorize the work.

You don't see rainmaking as urgent. You don't see these potential clients as "real" relationships yet. So it falls to the bottom of the list.

*Be real:* if Taylor Swift called and wanted coffee, you'd move things around. You'd make it happen. So why can't you do that for your future? Why can't you give that same energy to building something that will actually change your career?

## Urgency vs. Impact

Urgency is loud. It shows up in all CAPS. It rings your phone. It slaps "*ASAP*" on everything.

But impact? *Impact is quiet.* It doesn't scream. It waits.

Which is why it gets ignored. You'll reschedule your own growth a thousand times before you cancel a call labeled "urgent." Truth: *urgency is other people's priorities. Impact is yours.*

## Start Small. Start Now.

Make a move, any move. Start messy. Just don't stay stuck.

You don't need a perfect system. You don't need to color-code your calendar or spend three hours making a list. You just need to do one thing today that moves a relationship forward. One email. One text. One DM. One five-minute conversation in the hallway that doesn't start with "How's your caseload?" That's it. That's rainmaking—in motion.

*You're not too busy. Treat this like it matters.*

## When You Have to Do More to Be Seen as Equal

Some of us carry more weight that others don't have to. You're not just juggling deadlines. You're navigating the constant pressure to prove you belong.

You show up twice as prepared. You get interrupted and talked over. You give origination credit away, so you're seen as a team player—and still get left out of the real decisions. You work harder just to be seen as *equally competent.*

Rainmaker: Unleashed

So when someone tells you to "just block time for rainmaking," it doesn't land. Because you're already overextended. Already exhausted. Always doing more.

That's why you have to protect your energy like it's part of your strategy. Not everything deserves your time. Not every request deserves your yes. And not every ask deserves an explanation.

*If the work isn't building your book, your relationships, or your reputation—it's stealing from your future.*

**The ULTIMATE undisputed fact:**
**Revenue is power.**
**You can star that.**
**Underline it.**
**It's the damn truth.**

It's the thing that changes everything. When you bring in work, you don't have to keep proving your worth in every meeting, every pitch, every email thread. You shift from asking for a seat to owning one. That's why this matters. Not just to grow your book—but to stop living at the mercy of someone else's judgment. You want real leverage? Build something they can't ignore.

## For the Ones Who've Had to Endure More Than Just Busy

Let me slow this down for a minute. Because if you're like me, none of this "optimize your time" talk hits right unless we name the rest of it.

I've been in the conference room. Strategy meetings. All men. I was the only woman at the table. No one was listening, so I raised my voice—just to be heard.

You know what happened?

Someone looked at me and said,
"Is it your time of the month?"

*That wasn't in the '90s. That was 2016.*

And yes—it still stings.

# Rainmaker: Unleashed

So yeah—when I talk about carving out time for rainmaking, I know it's not just about scheduling. It's about surviving. It's about showing up in spaces where your voice is either ignored or punished for being firm. Where you're asked to prove your value with a smile and no edge.

That kind of invisible work? It drains you before the real work even starts.

And then the second-guessing kicks in: *"Was I too direct? Should I have smiled more? Maybe I'm overreacting. Maybe I do need thicker skin."*

You replay the moment, wondering if it was your tone. Your words. Your presence. You start editing yourself—before anyone else even gets the chance. You'll leave meetings wondering if you imagined the tone. If maybe it *was* your fault. That's how the system stays intact. You start policing yourself so no one else has to.

And even when you say the right thing, in the right tone, at the right moment—it still doesn't land the same.
Not because it wasn't brilliant.
But because *you* said it.

And here I am, writing this years later.
**Guess what? It hurts all over again.**

I know you're tired. You've been tired. And now I'm asking you to do one more thing. But this one thing? It's for you. It's not to prove anything. It's not to survive the week. It's to make sure five years from now, you're not still asking permission to be heard. Make space anyway. You deserve more than survival.

*I'm not just writing this for me. I'm writing it for every one of us who's been told to quiet down, smile more, and stay grateful.*

## The Optics Parade

You know the routine.

You get brought into the pitch—not for your skills, not for your voice, but for the look of it. The visual. The "we get it" moment. You sit at the table. You nod at the right times. You drop a few lines of insight—just enough to check the box. And when the client signs on?

Rainmaker: Unleashed

The work goes to the usual crew.

You're not on the follow-up call. You're not looped into the staffing meeting. You're not the lead. You're the backdrop.

Because this wasn't about your value. It was about the *optics*.

And you sit there—calm on the outside, screaming on the inside.
Fuming in silence while wearing the perfect smile.
Because if you say anything, you can't control your emotions. And if you don't? You're complicit in your own erasure.

This isn't inclusion.
It's a performance.
And you were the prop.

## When Blame Still Lands on You

I once brought a C-suite executive from AmEx to lunch with my partners. He sat directly beneath the CEO. I had a real relationship with him—his family, his world. We'd gone to Chuck E. Cheese with his kids and played Whack-A-Mole. You know, the game where the heads pop up and you smack them with a foam hammer? That one.

This wasn't a LinkedIn connection. It was a real connection.

So I set it up. Made the introduction. Scheduled the lunch with the top partners in my firm. They never bothered to get to know me. But there they were—at that table—because *I* had the connection.

And after lunch?
They went to my boss and said I laughed inappropriately.

*Let me say that again: I brought them to the table.* They spent the entire meal talking about IP litigation—meanwhile, I *knew* my friend didn't give a damn about any of that. The GC handled it. The GC reported to *him*.

But I was the one who was inappropriate?

No one asked what mattered to the client. No one studied. No one prepared.
But suddenly *my* laugh was the takeaway.

And no—they didn't get the work.
Apparently, because of my laugh.

Not because they didn't prepare.
Not because they talked about IP litigation to someone who didn't care.
Not because they ignored my relationship with him.

**I laughed.**

That's what they remembered.
That's what they blamed.

*I've walked in these shoes. Fought the hard battles. And yet here I am.*

## When You're the Punchline *and* the Leverage

Another lunch. Five of us. I was the only woman at the table. The client—male, of course—only talked to me. Ignored the others. Every question, every comment—directed at me. He was clearly hitting on me. Everyone saw it. No one said a word.

We wrapped the lunch, walking back to the office. And one of the guys on my team—joking, always joking—said:

**"You need to take one for the team."**

They all laughed.

I didn't.

Because they knew.

They knew exactly what was happening. And instead of shutting it down, they rode it out—because it helped them. Because it made the lunch feel like a win. My colleagues thought it was funny to laugh at my expense.

It didn't matter that I was uncomfortable.
It didn't matter that it was demeaning.
As long as the client was happy, the rest didn't matter.

*This is what it looks like when your presence is seen as a tactic—not a teammate.*

## Why I'm Telling You This

You might be wondering why I'm sharing these awful stories.

*Because I remember every second.*
*Because I didn't have the luxury of forgetting.*
*They did.*

I know what it feels like to think you're the only one.

The only one who walked out of a client lunch feeling dirty.
The only one who got blamed for not being "polished" enough after doing all the work.
The only one who thought maybe—just maybe—it really was your fault.

You're not imagining it.
You're not overreacting.
And you're not alone.

I'm telling you these stories because I wish someone had told them to me—back when I was sitting in silence, thinking maybe I just wasn't built for this. **But I was. And so are you.**

And if these stories sound familiar?
*Then you already know why rainmaking isn't optional.*
*It's the one part of this job where they don't get to decide your value.*
**You do.**

## The Power That Is Only Yours

This is the part no one can steal. No one can take credit for. No one can explain away.

When you build relationships that lead to revenue—*that's yours.* Not because someone gave you a shot. Not because you played the game right. Because you showed up, again and again, even when it hurt.

No one can minimize your ideas. Undercut your voice. Question your presence. They can't erase the work you bring in. No one can gatekeep clients who chose *you.* They can't take origination credit if you never invited them in the first place.

That's the power.
That's the difference.
That's why this chapter exists.

Because when the work is yours—*you* get to decide how loud you are.
You don't need permission anymore.
You don't need to be palatable.
You don't need to laugh at their jokes.

**You just need to own what you've built—and never give it back.**

**You've survived the bullshit.**

*Now let's burn the blueprint and write your own.*

# Chapter 17

# How Freedom Is Built

If Chapter 16 made you uncomfortable—good. That's what it feels like to sit in the truth, it doesn't get softened for your comfort. And if those stories weren't your stories? That doesn't mean you're off the hook. It means you're in a system that lets that slide—and counts on your silence to keep it that way. Now that it's out in the open, what are you going to do with it?

*Because here's the truth:* no matter where you sit in this hierarchy, the moment you stop reacting and start getting intentional—about your clients, your time, your name—you stop playing defense. You start building leverage. You want power? ***It begins here.***

You don't just stumble into freedom. You build it—intentionally, ruthlessly, and with receipts. If you think this is where we coast, you haven't been paying attention.

*The goal was never just to have power—it's to use it.*

Because power without structure?
It burns out. Fast.

This is where you draw the line. No more begging. No more proving. No more hoping the work gets noticed. *You finally know: the work doesn't speak for itself—you do.*

Because if you grew up like me, that was the phrase you heard. On repeat.

**"The work speaks for itself."**
That was the Patel family mantra. Do your part. Keep your head down. Don't ask for credit—just deliver. You'll be recognized. My mom drilled that into me. It wasn't advice. It was expectation.

*Spoiler: It doesn't.*

And I believed it. For a long time.

What I've learned: ***The work doesn't speak for itself. People do.*** And the ones who speak—who advocate, who position, who make sure they're seen—those are the ones who move up. I've watched mediocre people get promoted simply because they were louder about their accomplishments than I ever was.

*That's not bitterness. That's data.*

You're not just trying to get clients. You're building something that makes you untouchable.

*And freedom? It's not a vibe. It's a system.*

## It Starts with Your Roster

Most attorneys build their client list the way people have junk drawers—by accident.

A few referrals, a favor to a friend, some random inbound that felt flattering at the time. Before you know it, you've got a practice full of people you never actually meant to serve.

*That ends here.* Your roster isn't just a list—it's your strategy. Every name on it either makes you sharper or drags you sideways.

*If you wouldn't want to clone them, why are you still sending them Holiday cards?*

This isn't about being cold. It's about being clear. The more intentional you are about who gets your time, the less you have to explain your value. Because when your clients reflect your worth, you don't just earn more—you breathe easier. That's not selfish. That's sustainable.

### Your Best Clients Are a Blueprint

If you want more freedom, look at the clients who already give it to you. The ones who respect your time. Who ask smart questions. Who make you sharper because they trust you enough to let you lead. *That's not luck—that's just facts.*

Audit your best clients. What industry are they in? What kind of personalities do they have? Who referred them? What do they have in common? Because once the pattern emerges, you stop guessing—and you start replicating.

And don't just look at revenue. Look at how you feel after the call. Look at who refers you without being asked. Look at who pays on time without the drama. Those patterns matter. Because when your clients match your energy, your values, and your style? You don't just do better work—you protect your energy without even trying. That's not just alignment. That's insulation.

*Freedom gets easier when you stop reinventing and start repeating what already works.*

## Retention Is a Power Play

Everyone's out here chasing new clients like it's a sport. But the smartest rainmakers? They're doubling down on the ones they've already earned.

*Retention isn't reactive—it's leverage.* It's where trust compounds. It's where the real work happens—work that goes deeper, feels easier, and leads to better results. Because when the relationship isn't new, you stop proving yourself—and start expanding the possibilities.

Look at the biggest rainmakers in New York. Their client relationships aren't transactional—they're lifelong. Their families vacation together. They go to each other's milestone events. And you know what else? They're almost always the lead partner on those $50 million accounts.

How'd they get there? Not by chasing. By staying. By showing up consistently, delivering with substance, and being the first call when it matters most. That's not luck. That's what happens when you invest in a client long enough for the work to stop being just work.

*Stop chasing. Start deepening. That's the real flex.*

## Friends Refer. Clients Don't.

Referrals don't come from satisfied clients. They come from invested ones. The kind who trust you enough to put their own name behind yours.

*Hard truth:* most attorneys mistake politeness for loyalty. Just because someone likes your work doesn't mean they'll send you business.

**Want referrals? Are they invested in your success? Are you theirs?**

Build relationships that go deeper than the matter. Show up when there's nothing on the table. Make it personal. Because people don't refer professionals—they refer people they like, trust, and want to see win.

***That's the difference between being someone's lawyer—and being someone they listen to.***

- ✓ *Their consigliere.*
- ✓ *When it matters.*
- ✓ *When it's messy.*
- ✓ *When no one else is in the room.*

And while we're here—know the difference between influence and authority. Some clients can say yes. Others make sure you're at the table. You need both. The decision-maker controls the budget. But the influencer? They're your internal hype man. The one who edifies you not only as a person but your value. The one who smooths the politics. If you've got someone who champions you from the inside—and someone with the power to say yes? That's the combo that builds empires. It also grows your footprint inside that company.

***There's only 24 hours in a day. Don't Scale Yourself. Scale Your Impact.***

There aren't enough hours in the day. You need sleep too. You need to protect the time that only *you* can spend. The highest-performing attorneys aren't doing more. They're just doing less of what drains them. Less admin. Less chasing. Less explaining.

Want more freedom? Start protecting your sharpest hours. Use tech to stay visible. Build habits that keep relationships warm without faking it. Because when you treat your attention like a limited asset—it starts paying you back like one.

## You Don't Just Practice on Clients

You want to build freedom? Practice the skill before you need it.

# Rainmaker: Unleashed

Rainmaking isn't something you suddenly "turn on" the day you get promoted or land a client-facing role. It's not a script. It's a muscle. And the only way to get good at it—*really good*—is to start practicing when the stakes are low.

Practice with your friends and family.
Practice with your dentist.
Practice with your kid's soccer coach.
Practice at dinner with someone you've known for years.

*Why?* Zero risk. Because those are the people who already trust you. You don't have to perform. You just have to *connect*.

One of my clients started practicing on everyone in his life. His wife looked at him one day and said, *"Wow, you're becoming more social."*

Ask better questions. Follow up on the things they care about. Offer help when it's not expected. Learn to read energy, not just the words. See how people respond. Get used to what it feels like when you're fully present, *not selling,* and still making a lasting impression.

That's the real training ground. Not for the win—for the flex.

When you're practicing with people who already trust you? *You're not rehearsing. You're rewiring.* And if you're only "on" when a client's in front of you? You'll always be chasing the moment instead of building momentum.

**Practice everywhere and anywhere—until it becomes second nature.** *So when the big opportunity comes? You're already ready.*

After the pandemic—and two knee replacements—I realized something that hit hard. I didn't know anyone within two blocks who could help if something went wrong. And I didn't want to feel that isolated again.

I made a decision: I was going to build relationships with my neighbors. I showed up at the pool. The monthly comedy nights. I started conversations, remembered names, followed up. Eventually, the group got too big for individual texts—so I created a WhatsApp thread.

Now? That thread is thriving. We help each other. We go out for a drink, late-night emergencies, awkward dating stories. I never run out of people who can show up when I need it.

Rainmaker: Unleashed

That's the thing: **That's rainmaking too.**

It's not about being "on." It's about being *intentional.*

Building relationships isn't something you save for clients. It's something you practice everywhere. With everyone. Because when it's second nature in your personal life, it becomes effortless in your professional one.

*When that happens? You don't just make rain. You build weather systems.*

Now that you've built the skill—Let me show you how to save time using it. While you can't scale relationships, **you can scale the hell out of your time.**

## AI Is Your Best Associate

You don't need another body on your team burning hours writing LinkedIn posts, scrambling to prep CLEs, or drafting those "just circling back" emails. You've already got one—and it's faster, sharper, and doesn't bill your clients. AI isn't a gimmick. It's leverage. Used right, it can give you back weeks of your life. It can help you prep smarter, write cleaner, research companies in minutes, and show up consistently without handing your voice to the marketing department. Honestly, most of those departments aren't built for speed or results anyway. AI is. You just have to know how to prompt it.

Used right, AI becomes your clarity tool. It helps you get the first draft down fast, so you're not burning energy staring at a blank screen or obsessing over the perfect opener.

*Again, it doesn't replace your voice—it gives it a head start.*

And let's be clear—*AI won't replace your legal judgment. It won't write your case briefs or interpret statutes.* But it can help you write CLEs, LinkedIn posts, emails, and thought leadership that actually sounds like you. It gives you back time—and protects your energy for the stuff that matters.

*You don't need a team. You need a system.*

When you learn how to use AI right? You show up more, respond faster, and stay visible—without begging marketing for approval or hiring help to sound like you.

This isn't about replacing thinking. It's about removing friction. The time you used to spend on mental gymnastics—"what do I say, how do I start, what if it sounds off"—that's now five minutes and done. That's the difference between *knowing* what to do and actually doing it. AI helps you close that gap.

If you train your AI properly, it gets you 90% of the way there. Then you tweak. That's it. It's like Google back in the day— you learned it or got left behind. Same thing now.

This isn't about mastering a tool. It's about deciding whether you want to move faster, sound sharper, and actually get things done—or keep pretending you don't have time. *Less sleep for you.*

### *When You Get This Right, Freedom Follows*
You don't need 100 clients. You need the right ones. The ones who pay you well, refer you often, and never make you explain your value.

*And it's not about more hours—it's about fewer time-wasters.*

You need boundaries.

And you don't need a team of marketing folks and associates to stay visible—that'll take you months.

### *You need a system built for speed—not approval.*

Because when you filter your energy, eliminate the noise, and use your tools like a weapon? You buy back hours, protect your name, and stop scrambling just to keep up. That's when everything shifts. You're no longer waiting to be chosen. You're choosing who gets access.

*That's what freedom looks like. And you built it.*

### *Okay—so what if you're the associate I just roasted?*
The one ghostwriting LinkedIn posts for someone else. The one running around collecting bios, drafting CLE outlines, or "circling back" for the fifteenth time while your name barely makes it on the pitch.

Rainmaker: Unleashed

Don't panic. Just stay with me.

*Because this next chapter?*
*It's what no one's telling you—but absolutely should be.*

# Chapter 18

Rainmaker: Unleashed

# Associates – Your Secret Sauce

Let's just lay it out there... Most partners don't want you to know what's in this chapter.

Not because you're not ready—but because the system is designed to keep you dependent. Keep your head down. Keep proving yourself while someone else takes the credit. That's the ladder. Not everyone makes partner—and the fewer who rise, the more power stays concentrated at the top.

**Truth: associates are the most underestimated asset in the firm.**

You have access. You have proximity. You work with clients. You sit in the meetings. You write the drafts. You're on the emails.

*You don't even realize it—but you have more touchpoints than anyone else.* More than the partners.

**If you know how?**

How to build credibility early and intentionally? You stop waiting for someone to give you permission. You start building something that no one can take away.

And you don't have to start from scratch. The beginning of your client base? It's already in your orbit.

## Start with the Network You Already Have

Your future client list? You already know half of them. Law school classmates. Undergrad friends. People you partied with who are now in tech, finance, real estate, startups.

**Shhh... here's a little secret:** *everybody is somebody in twenty years.*

And with LinkedIn, you don't have to guess who's going where—you can watch it happen in real time. Most associates treat LinkedIn like a job board. But it's not—it's your living, breathing rolodex. You can see when someone switches jobs. You can like a post, comment, send a quick DM. And while others are burning out or hiding from networking, you're building quiet momentum. You don't need anything now. That's the point. But five years from now? Ten? When your name is up for partner? They'll want to help—because they've been with you through your whole journey.

*And you've been there for theirs.*

### Keep Your Eye on Who Has the Clients

Want to know who actually has power in your firm? They're not in the office. Don't look at who talks the most in meetings. Look at the signature line. Who's emailing the client directly? Who's listed as lead partner on the case? Who's setting the tone on calls—even when they're not physically there?

Most associates think they'll learn how rainmaking works by watching the people around them in the office. But the top rainmakers? You barely see them. They're not camped out in a glass office—they're jumping on calls between golf rounds, flying out for client meetings, grabbing drinks or lunch, or getting looped in at the last minute because the client insisted on them. If you only study the structure inside your practice group, you'll miss the power that's actually driving the firm.

*The influence isn't always seen. But the email chains never lie.*

### Get Close to the Rainmakers

Everything in this book? It still applies to you. The difference is—if you're reading this now as an associate? You get to start earlier than the rest of us did. You get to build the habits before it's high stakes. You get to practice while everyone else is still "heads down" hoping good work gets noticed.

Apply the skills in this book to the people who can actually move your career forward. The rainmakers. The ones who will get you promoted—or open the door to your next job. Build and strengthen those relationships the same way you would with trusted mentors—*intentionally, consistently, and with something real behind it.*

And don't wait for some magical client opportunity to start practicing.

Start with your friends. Your classmates. Your peer group.

Rainmaker: Unleashed

Learn how to stay in touch, how to follow up, how to make yourself memorable without performing.

This should've been taught in law school—but it wasn't.

*And you paid six figures for that education.* **This one's free.**

## Make Sure the Client Knows *You*

Want to build a book of clients? Start by making sure the current clients know your name. Not the firm's. Not just the partner's. **Yours.**

The biggest mistake associates make? Thinking it's not their place. Thinking they're too junior to matter. But the smartest thing you can do is quietly build trust with every client you touch—even if your role is small. That's how reputations are built. That's how relationships are earned.

My brother Amit became one of the youngest partners at EY—not because he politicked his way there, but because he understood one thing early: the client needed to know *him*. I was in his ear the whole time—telling him to show up, speak up, and make sure the relationship didn't live or die with the lead. That advice changed his career.

And if you get offered a secondment? ***Go.***

Most associates dread it—but if you know what you're doing, it's your golden ticket.

Take them to lunch. Grab drinks. Hang out. Ask smart questions. Learn their business.

Find out what they're working toward—professionally and personally. ***Help them.***

*Show up like someone who gives a damn.* And then? *Stay in touch.* Get introduced to more people. Keep the momentum going.

Because here's the truth no one tells you:
***Again every single one of those client contacts will be somebody in 15–20 years.***
*Some of them in five.*

And if you were the associate they trusted, listened to, and remembered? You just built the foundation of your future client base—without ever making a pitch. Just with trust and likability. Who knew?

## If You Can't Find a Mentor—Go Get One

Not every firm is generous with mentorship. Some partners are genuinely too busy. Others hoard clients, guard relationships, and treat associates like staffing widgets.

If that's your reality? ***Don't wait for help. Go get it.***

Join a bar association. Volunteer with a nonprofit. There are Young Lawyers groups everywhere—like the *New York State Bar Association's Young Lawyers Section,* open to attorneys under 37 or in their first 10 years of practice. And don't overlook the *minority bar associations*—they are powerful, built-in communities that will lift you while you grow.

Early in my career, I served on the board of the South Asian Bar Association of New York, and the people I met there? They're still in my life. Some became champions. Some became lifelong friends.

Those relationships didn't come from chasing—they came from showing up.

These groups aren't just résumé fillers.
They're ***relationship engines.***

### Get Involved
You'll meet GCs. Associates at other firms. Judges. Future clients. And maybe—someone who'll take an interest in your path. Or you'll find your next job.

That's your external bench.
Build it now. Nurture it forever.
Because when the system doesn't pick you? You still have power.
***You pick yourself. Get to it.***

And while you're building that bench? Don't forget to build your name. Because relationships open doors—but your reputation decides who walks through them.

## Brand Yourself Early

LinkedIn isn't just for job hunting. It's not just for lawyers switching firms or firms announcing wins. It's the easiest way to show the world what you care about—without shouting.

If you want to be remembered when it matters, start showing up now. Comment on a post. Share a CLE. Say something useful. Say something real. You don't need to be a thought leader. Just show that you *think*.

And here's your first move:
**Add everyone you meet to LinkedIn. Starting now.**
Opposing counsel. Summer associates. People from court. That CLE speaker you liked. You don't need a reason. You just need to stay connected.

But don't stop at digital. This isn't about building an "online presence"—it's about being known, remembered, and *real*.

Join LinkedIn groups for young lawyers in your city. Go to events. Grab a drink. Talk to people who aren't in your office.

*Go to concerts. Start an intramural team. Be the social chair.*
Yes, really.

Those moments—those connections—are where trust is built. Not in a pitch meeting. Not on a client call. But when you're the one who made it easy for people to show up and belong.

And if you're in a city where none of that exists? **Start it.** People remember the person who made things happen. Not the one who waited for an invitation.

*Here's the part most people miss: You can publish articles on LinkedIn. About music. About mindset. About your dog.*

It doesn't have to be about work—it just has to be *you*.

Ten years from now, one of those names will be a GC. Somebody else will become a client. And if they already know you—because they played softball with you or liked your LinkedIn post last month? You won't have to sell them on anything. You'll already be someone they trust.

People are already looking at your profile. They're already making assumptions. They're already deciding if they'd want to work with you—or work for you.

So let them find someone strategic.
Someone thoughtful.
Someone who quietly built a presence before the title ever showed up. The key on LinkedIn is personality. We covered that earlier in the book. Post like a real person—not with blank reposts.

You don't need a brand that performs. You need one that connects.
Brand yourself early.

I'll be honest. If you're reading this, I'm jealous.
Because I wish someone had told the 25-year-old version of me.

**You got this.**

And for the women reading this—especially the ones who've been told to wait their turn, keep their head down, or be "more polished"?
*You're up next.*

*Let's talk about what happens when the system doesn't expect you to lead— and you do it anyway.*

# Chapter 19

# It's Not Confidence. It's Knowing My Value.

Have you ever sat in a conference room and had this thought:
*"I might be smarter than everyone in here. Wow... I actually am."*

Over the course of my career, I've sat at those tables listening to mansplaining on a loop. I'd say an idea—no reaction. Then the guy next to me repeats it out loud, and suddenly? It's *brilliant.* He gets the credit. (Too bad he never knows how to implement *my* idea.) Ha!

It's those **holy shit** moments that stack up over time.
The ones that made me realize: I don't need to keep asking for a seat. I needed to build my own table.

That's why I started Sage Ivy.
Apparently I have a problem with authority.
Correction: *I am* the authority.

Let's dig in. About how I can empower you the same way. Because this next part? It's the truth they don't put in training manuals.

*It's what I wish someone told me, decades ago.*

## You're Already Overqualified

One more credential. One more white paper. One more certification...

**Stop.**

Those things look great on a résumé, but let's be honest—the ultimate credential is *revenue.* By this point in the book, you should've seen that coming.

What I've hinted at before: whether it's imposter syndrome, or the polite lies we've been told about what else it's going to take to "earn it," it all leads to the same trap—*delay.*

Facts? Women are better at EQ—emotional intelligence—than men. We are. But no one ever taught us how to leverage that into revenue.

Rainmaker: Unleashed

Let's talk about it.

*What is EQ?*

It's knowing who not to trust.
It's knowing who your real friends are.
It's knowing who your "Go-To" is when you want to bitch about something.
It's the people who show up without being asked.
It's the ones who say, *"I've got you,"* and actually mean it.

It's people who cheer for your successes without jealousy.

**Now take that.** *Apply it to clients.*

Throughout this book, I've talked about building strong, untouchable relationships. Another fact: *you already know how to do this.* You already have this muscle fully activated. You just haven't thought about it in this context.

*Until now.*

This isn't new. You already know how to read the room—wait, scratch that—you already know how to read the people.

You can tell when someone's off. When they're faking nice.
*Mean girls? Please.* You saw it coming before they smiled.

You catch when they're checked out.
When they're testing you.
*Sketchy guys?* Your gut clocked them before your brain did.

Your B.S. radar?
**Always on.**

*That's EQ in motion*—and exactly what it takes to build real client trust.

Rainmaking isn't about slick pitches or flawless decks. It's about seeing what the client actually needs—even when they don't say it. It's remembering that their son just started college. That their dad's in hospice. That their tone changed when the GC got on the call.

That's not "soft skills." That's strategy.
That's how trust is built—and how decisions get made.

You've been doing this your whole life.
Now it's time to stop thinking of it as just your personality—you're a giver or a pleaser—and start treating it like a ***superpower***.

## You'll Get Knocked Down. Hard.

*I had a friend—someone I'd known for over seven years. A partner at a law firm. He kept asking for my ideas. Big ones.*

*So I gave them to him. I told him what I saw—gaps in the "business" of law firms. The holes no one else was naming. I laid out a structure I believed in—something new.*

*I see the business differently—the cracks in the model, the patterns hiding in plain sight, the opportunities no one's naming yet.*

*He listened. Then asked me to write a piece of the proposal he was submitting to leadership. I did. They approved it.*

*Then he asked me to write the job description.*
*I did that too.*

*In my mind, I was writing my own job description. And when the role was finally created? He told me I'd have to apply like everyone else. "No problem." Surely he's going to tell the hiring committee that this is my brainchild.*

*Instead he said, "We don't want it to look like nepotism." Nepotism?*

*I created the entire concept. From scratch. With zero credit.*

*They hired someone else. She lasted three months.*
*Oh, he had the nerve to ask me to reapply.*
**Hell to the No.**

*He got promoted to the firm's management committee.*
*Bought a second house.*

Rainmaker: Unleashed

*And when I asked him later to support Sage Ivy?*
*He said no. The firm had already spent the budget—on my idea. (I think he was afraid I'd expose him.)*

I never spoke to him again.

Yeah—I'm still angry.
Because it wasn't just a job. It was my stolen *vision*.
And I watched someone else co-opt it and use it to climb while I got ghosted from my own work.

I still give grace—even after the first hit.
But once the pattern's clear? Door closed. For good.

Why this story? Because it happens all the time. To women like me. To people like you. You can have the ideas, the talent, the relationships—and still be erased when it's time to give credit. Ego gets in the way– *not yours.*

I want you to see it before it happens. To trust your gut when someone keeps asking for more but never offers anything back. To stop assuming that loyalty will be repaid just because it should be.

This isn't just a cautionary tale. It's a line in the sand. Own your work. Protect your vision. Recognize the pattern. Because the moment you stop giving your brilliance away for free—everything changes.

I know my value now. I earned it—with scars. **You don't have to.**

## The Cost of Being Seen

I had a partner who refused to learn my name.
Not *didn't know it—refused.*

We were at a conference, and she saw how many people I knew. Suddenly, she wanted introductions.

I was at the hotel bar with a longtime friend—someone I'd stayed close with since law school. We were still joking like we were twenty-five. She came up behind me and said loud enough for everyone to hear: "Se-hal, introduce me to your friend."

He turned around. Deadpan.
"First, it's Sejal. Second, I run legal for a global financial institution. And you're interrupting."

The bar went silent.
She was embarrassed.

So she wrote me up.
Put me on probation.

Why?
Because I had too much presence.
Too many connections.
And the audacity to be seen.

## How Women Show Up

It doesn't always start with trust. Or warmth. Or even basic respect. Sometimes you show up—and they punish you for being visible.

One of the strongest relationships in my life didn't start as a friendship. Beth and I were just colleagues. I didn't trust her at first—I don't usually trust anyone I work with. But somewhere along the way, she became my rock.

The thing that sets her apart: she doesn't just say she'll introduce me to people—she actually does it. She follows through. She makes the email intro. She opens doors. She brings my name up even if I'm not there.

Beth's the reason I got one of my recent speaking engagements. *She's that person who makes it happen—whatever it is.*

That's not casual friendship. That's strategic trust. Because most people are friendly, but not invested. They like you, but they're not thinking about your success when they walk away from a conversation.

**We do this together.** We invest in each other and lift each other up. With work. With life. Beth is different. *She shows up like your wins are hers too.*

## Rainmaker: Unleashed

And that's what rainmaking relationships really look like—people who move like they're in it with you, and whose names you carry forward just as hard.

When you find that? Don't just be grateful. ***Be reciprocal. This isn't networking. This is co-investment.***

Let's be honest—there's another side to this. How many times have you had a conversation about that woman? The one who finally made it to the top. The one who broke through. The one who had to fight for her seat—and now guards it like it's the last one left.

She doesn't promote other women. She doesn't mentor. She doesn't open doors. She doesn't just withhold—she knifes you.

Why? Because she's afraid she'll lose her spot. Because someone made her believe there's only room at the table for only one of us.

***My take? Make a bigger damn table!***

I've known both kinds of women. The ones who move with you—and the ones who are against you. Some do it to protect their spot. Some just never learned how to invest in anyone but themselves.

The women who rise and bring others with them? They realize that other women are allies. ***They're the ones who build something that actually lasts.*** That's who I want around me. That's who I want you to be—women who back each other with intention, not applause.

I'm not telling you anything you don't know. We've all met both.

You don't need every woman to support you.
But the ones who do? *You build with them.*
Because rainmaking isn't about going it alone. It's about knowing who walks beside you—and who's holding the damn door. It takes a village. Good news, you know how to build that village already.

You've done the work. You've owned your value. You've seen how trust is built—and how fast it can be broken. You've felt what it's like when someone advocates for you. And what it's like when someone conveniently forgets you were the one who made it all happen.

***You already have all the tools inside you. Use them.***

But now we're moving into the part no one prepares you for:
What happens after you've made the connection? After the client is interested?
When you're no longer just delivering the work—but shaping the relationship?

Because you can't win the game if you don't understand who's holding the ball.

Most lawyers? Have no idea what in-house counsel actually notice.

***Time to change that.***

Rainmaker: Unleashed

# Chapter 20

# The Inside Scoop
## *(formerly known as The Mysterious Client)*

Throughout this book, we've been chasing a mysterious figure:

***"The client."***

We plan. We prep. We try to impress—but not look desperate. Be useful—but not overstep. Like we're auditioning for someone we've never met. Like this person is some kind of unicorn we're all trying to hook with LinkedIn posts and lunch invitations.

Plot twist: *They're human, too.*

They're juggling 40 matters, 12 internal meetings, 3 budget cuts, and at least one exec who treats them like a concierge. They don't have time for performative nonsense—or "just checking in" emails that say nothing.

So let's stop treating this like a royal courtship.

*Let's talk about what actually matters to them—how they think, how they decide who to hire, and what makes them say, "Let's bring this person in."*

Being good at what you do? That's expected.

(No one's giving out trophies.)

*But that's the starting line—not the win.*

## What In-House Counsel Actually Pays Attention To

So if being smart and available isn't the differentiator, what is?

In-house counsel aren't impressed by your law school ranking or your 47-page CV. They're managing internal politics, outside pressure, shrinking budgets, and executives who want everything yesterday. They're not looking for someone who dazzles.

They want someone who delivers.

Rainmaker: Unleashed

Paul Grewal, Chief Legal Officer of Coinbase, once said it plainly:

*"Most lawyers delude themselves into thinking they win client loyalty through expertise. In reality, their only chance is through unique responsiveness and attention to detail."*

**That's not just a hot take—it's a wake-up call.**
**Because even when lawyers are responsive, they still miss the mark.**

You know what drives in-house counsel up the wall? When outside counsel gives a clear answer on the phone—then buries it in a legal opinion full of caveats. What felt like guidance turns into a hedge. Suddenly the opinion they trusted disappears under layers of legal disclaimers. It doesn't feel careful. It feels like you're covering your ass. And next time? They won't call you first.

Paul's pointing to what happens when lawyers get stuck in commodity mode. He's not wrong. It's the fallout from a broken system—where no one teaches you how to build trust before the work even starts. It's a reality check. But it's not a roadmap.

That's where this chapter steps in.

This is where most lawyers stall out. They've got the skills—but no roadmap for how to create the kind of trust that makes responsiveness actually land. Because when trust is real, you're not just answering emails.

*You're already inside. You've earned it. That changes everything.*

## Slow Down

You get an email at 10:42 am. asking for a quick legal read. So you drop what you're doing, crank out a response in record time, and hit send by 11:03. Fast. Efficient. Done.

*Silence.*

Because here's what no one tells you: *speed isn't responsiveness.* Especially when there's no relationship.

Without trust, your lightning-fast reply looks rushed. Generic. Maybe even risky.

But when the relationship is real? You're not scrambling to prove yourself. You're thinking clearly. You've seen this person under pressure before. You know what tone they need, how much context they expect, and when to cut the *legal caveats and just say what you think.*

And if something's off? You pick up the phone.

"Saw your note. Want to walk me through what you're up against so I can get you what you actually need?"

That's responsiveness.

*Not fast. On point. Not reactive. Strategic. It's the difference between being available—and being indispensable.*

### Who's Actually Reading This?

Here's how it usually goes. In-house sends a question. You fire off a clean legal answer. No context. No idea who else is reading it. You're flying blind—and hoping it lands.

But when you've got real access? It plays out differently.

They pick up the phone.

"Hey—I'm about to forward this to our CFO. Here's what I'm trying to accomplish."

Now you're not guessing. You've got direction. You're not writing into the void—you're writing with purpose. You know the audience, the stakes, and how your words will be used. That's the inside track. And it doesn't come from brilliance. It comes from trust you've earned.

*That's the shift—from outside help to inside edge. From someone they hire... to someone they lean on.*

### It's Their World. Learn It.

You're on a pitch call. A partner starts reading their résumé out loud. "Fifteen years in complex litigation... Young Lawyer accolades...

Former clerk…" In-house counsel is nodding—while scrolling through email.

None of that matters if you don't get *their* problem.

They're not hiring you to get up to speed. They've already got smart lawyers. What they need is someone who gets the pressure they're under—and knows how to help them move fast.

Useless overstaffing will kill trust FAST. When five associates show up and only one contributes, in-house sees exactly what's happening. The rest are there to pad the bill. The $800/hour note-taking. That's not support—it's theater. And it pisses them off.

Now imagine this:

You're on that same call. And instead of listing credentials, you say: "We saw something similar in a product risk matter in your space—want to hear how we handled it?"

That lands. That's relevance. Now your experience isn't a list—it's a shortcut.

Because when they trust that you *already understand* what they're dealing with, they don't need to read your bio. They don't just hire you—*they hire a trusted advisor.*

## You're Either the Shortcut—or the Delay.

AGC emails you on a Thursday afternoon: "Can we terminate this agreement without triggering penalties?"

Sure—you could write 500 words, quote the clause, and lay out every legal angle. But if you've got real context? You already know that's not what they're really asking.

You call.

"Is this political, or financial?"

They pause. "Financial. We're cleaning up spend before end of quarter."

Rainmaker: Unleashed

Now you know exactly what your advice needs to do: *protect them—and help them hit the number.* So instead of a memo, you send a one-pager: clear options, risk levels, and a call they can walk into their next ops meeting ready to make.

You just saved them a redline war, a two-week delay, and the embarrassment of looping in legal too late. You kept them out of the fire—and they remember that.

That's the benefit. Not what you know—what you prevent.

***Clients remember the lawyers who keep them out of messes.***

The real edge: when you understand your client's personal and professional goals, they'll tell you everything. The politics. The pressure points. What the C-suite actually cares about. And most importantly—how to make them look good. That's your advantage.

And you don't get that access by asking. Not by being louder. Or flashier. You earn it by being the one who sees around corners. Who stays steady when everyone else is spinning. The one who makes the next move obvious—before they even ask for it.

The ones who don't waste words. Who say just enough—then stop. That's who in-house starts to rely on. Not just as outside help. As the call they make under pressure.

***The one they want in the foxhole.***

Here's what actually moves the needle: *the relationships you've built, the results you've delivered, and the way people vouch for you when you're not in the room.* That's what moves you past the process.

*Here's what actually matters:*

- ✓ *The relationships you've built.*
- ✓ *The results you've delivered.*
- ✓ *And the way people vouch for you when you're not in the room.*

Preferred provider lists? They exist. Of course they do. But most in-house lawyers have room to go outside them—and they do. Especially

Rainmaker: Unleashed

when you've already proven your value. Especially when working with you makes their job easier. The strongest relationships don't get buried in process. They get fast-tracked.

## The Power of "I Don't Know"

Confidence isn't knowing everything. It's knowing when to shut up and say, "I'll find out." It's about owning what you don't know. When you try to fake it, they feel it. You ramble. You hedge. You wrap the truth in disclaimers. Or worse—you lie about what you can do.

**You quickly establish trust with 3 words.**

And the client starts wondering what else you're spinning. What else are you going to lie about in the future? *You broke trust.*

But when you say, *"I don't know, but I'll find out,"* you reset the room. You're not guessing. You're human—and clients appreciate it.

In-house counsel doesn't expect you to know everything. They expect you to tell the truth—quickly. And to get them what they need without a side of ego.

The lawyers who say "I don't know" early? They're the ones who get the call when the stakes are high—because they're not afraid of the truth. They *work with it.*

## No Surprises. No Bullshit.

**You want to tank trust in under 60 seconds? Surprise them on billing. (Highlight that and Red Flag it.)**

You know what breaks trust before the work even starts? When law firms are negotiating the matter—and bring up expensing dinners, rides, and car service for their associates. If your partner rate is $2,000 an hour, that conversation should never happen. It sends the message that you're trying to squeeze every dollar, not solve the problem. And it annoys in-house before you've even earned the relationship.

And what happens if you try to sneak those charges in later without a heads-up?

If the GC finds out about an overage from their CFO, it doesn't matter how good the work was. You're already flagged.

No one wants to chase you for clarity. No one wants to have to try and explain your invoice in a finance meeting. And no one forgets the lawyer who made them look sloppy in front of their boss.

Communicate! Talk to your team, send weekly updates to the client. If the bill's going to hurt, the heads-up better come first. Not when the invoice lands. Not when the questions start. Before.

Because what clients remember isn't always the quality of the work. It's the feeling they had when they opened the bill. You'll kill all the capital you worked so hard to create.

## What You Can Do Right Now

If it's a current client, deepen it. Reach out with something useful. Ask what they're focused on. Ask what happens if the landscape shifts—regulations, priorities, leadership. Ask what's keeping the GC up at night.

You're not just making conversation—you're gathering context. So the next time they call, you're not starting from zero. You already know what matters.

If you're not on their radar yet, stop sending "hope you're well" emails. Start paying attention. Research. Study. Set up Google alerts for their company. Did they speak on a panel? Comment on a post? Get quoted in an article? Follow up with something specific. "Saw your quote in Bloomberg—are you seeing that issue come up more often internally? This is how I dealt with it for another client."

That shows strategic thinking. That starts conversations.

*And when that moment comes—the 'do you know someone?' moment—you're not an option. You're already the answer.*

## Shoutout to the Client's Power

*Clients have power most of them never use. Totally understated.*

Ms. In-house Counsel, you get to ask who's on the team. You get to say, "We'd love to see someone new in the pitch." You get to push for fresh faces—not just the same four people who always show up.

*Use your influence to empower.*

Outside counsel listens when money's on the line. Mic Drop. And the lawyers you elevate? They remember who gave them a shot. Who made space. Who asked for them by name.

*So ask.*

Ask who's getting visibility. Ask who's actually doing the work. Ask who's getting the credit. The best clients don't just direct matters. They *develop people.*

**That's power. Quiet. Intentional. Permanent.**

One question still dangling in the air. The kind no one answers directly. *But…whispered at lunches.*

# Chapter 21

# Origination = Power

**Origination is power.**
It's not a bonus. It's not a metric. It's the whole damn game.
*Because making partner doesn't mean you're in control.*
Not unless your name is on the client.

It's the difference between being seen as valuable and being seen as replaceable. If you're not getting origination credit, you're not building power—you're just billing hours.

This is what attorneys chase, whether they admit it or not. It determines who gets promoted, who gets protected, and who gets to walk into a room knowing they can't be ignored.

And yet, most firms treat it like a secret handshake—reserved for the partners already inside the circle. By the time they explain how it actually works, you may already have been left out of the deals that mattered.

You want control? Credit? Leverage?
*Origination is the gate.* And firms don't hand out the key.
They guard it. Gatekeep it. Weaponize it.
And by the time they tell you how it really works?
You're already behind.

## The Real Currency Is Origination Credit

Origination credit is the system law firms use to decide who gets rewarded for bringing in the client. Not who did the work. Not who managed the case. It's about who owns the client relationship. That's the engine behind most compensation decisions—even if other contributions get tracked. And in most firms? *That's the whole ballgame.*

*Whose relationship made the money walk through the door?*

And that answer shapes everything—from your compensation, to which committees you're placed on, to whether marketing even returns your emails.

Once your origination numbers hit a certain threshold, you get a little breathing room. You're safe... *until* next year, when the cycle begins anew.

There's no roadmap. No training. Origination credit isn't just a number—*it's protection.* Once your name is tied to enough revenue, they can't touch you. You're valuable.

But if your name's not on the client? You're a cost center. A line item. And when the next round of cuts comes? You're already on the list.

*And here's what no one tells you*: origination credit isn't just for work in your own practice. If you bring in a client and they hire your firm for something completely different—white collar, M&A, IP—you can still get credit. The percentages might vary, but the recognition is real.

Most attorneys have no idea. And when I ask my clients, how their firm tracks origination or pays it out, I get the same look—blank. They shrug. Then I make them go ask. *That's when the truth starts unraveling— quietly at first. And then it pisses them off.*

## Why No One Teaches It Until It's Too Late

You'd think something this important would be explained up front.
*It's not.*
It's not personal. It's just the part of the game no one teaches you—until you've already lost a round. It's just the kind of silence that protects the people who already know how it works.

Most firms aren't hiding anything. They're just not volunteering it.

*And if you don't know to ask? You won't.*

No one pulls you aside and explains how origination works—because they assume you'll figure it out. They did. If you don't? You miss it. And by the time you figure it out? It's already cost you.

So instead of teaching you, they let you guess.
And the ones who guess right? Move up. Others are moved out.

One of the reasons firms stay vague about origination? They don't want too many people asking.

Rainmaker: Unleashed

*Especially not associates.*

Associates are already elbowing each other to make partner—chasing the ring, thinking that's the finish line.

**But it's not. It's just the start of a whole new power structure.**

The firm will argue they're transparent. And it's true—*if* you ask. But what if you don't know to ask? What if you're the first in your family, your school, or your firm to get that far? What if you were taught to be excellent—not political?

Most attorneys don't ask—not because they don't care. Because they assume someone will tell them. And by the time they realize no one will? The credit's gone. And so is the leverage that came with it.

## Who's Really Getting the Credit?

You bring in the client, and you do the work. That's *direct origination*. Clean. Simple. In theory.

Where it gets sticky is when senior partners want in—under the guise of "training." Let's say you're going to lunch with your law school friend who happens to be in-house counsel. A senior partner asks to join—says it'll be good mentorship. At lunch, your friend casually mentions she's got a matter coming up and wants to send it your way.

**Who gets the credit?**

Not you. The senior partner takes it—because he was "training" you. That's how it works at a lot of firms.

I can't tell you how many friends have vented about stolen credit, awkward write-ups, and teammates who suddenly became the face of *their* relationships.

The kicker? You *could* fight for it. But you're still in an *associate mindset*—so you don't know you can.

**And here's the part most people miss:** origination isn't decided when the work starts. It's decided when the matter is created. Because the moment someone opens the matter, they're establishing the record—and that includes who gets listed as the relationship attorney.

Conflicts come *after* that. So if you're not driving the setup, not asserting your role when it's created, you're already at risk of being erased. Doesn't matter that you brought in the client. If your name's not on that matter from the jump, good luck reclaiming it later.

I had a client who didn't bring the senior partner—because I told him not to. But when the matter came in and he told the partner about it?

That same partner generously offered to open the matter and/or run conflicts. Guess who would've gotten origination—if I wasn't in his corner? *Exactly.*

*Lots of shady shit happens around origination.* Protecting yourself isn't optional. And trust me—some sketchy senior partners won't like how I suggest you do it.

But before we get there—let's talk about **indirect origination** and the other side of this equation.

## Do You Trust Your Colleagues With Your Clients?

*Indirect origination* sounds collaborative in theory. You bring in the relationship, but the actual work goes to another partner or practice group. You're told it's a win-win—you deepen the client relationship, and everyone wins.

Right?

Not always.

**The truth:** unless you've built internal relationships you trust, you just handed your client to someone who might write you out of the story. Most attorneys don't think about that risk. They focus so hard on building externally, they forget that internal strategy matters just as much.

First, you have to know this kind of credit even exists. The firm will hype it up—call it collaborative, good for growth, great for visibility. But

Rainmaker: Unleashed

underneath all that *'go team' energy?* If you're not strategic, you could lose the client.

Maybe not the first matter—but the next one.

And the one after that.

And then? You're no longer the relationship holder. You're the memory. Once another partner becomes the main point of contact, you're no longer essential. You opened the door. They moved in. *Quietly. Efficiently. Permanently.*

This is why we've been talking about client relationships the way we have—why the personal stuff isn't fluff. It's strategy. Make them laugh. Ask about their grandkid. Remember they're vegan. **When the relationship is real, no one gets to edge you out.**

That's why authentic relationships matter. When it is, the client won't just default to the other partner. They won't hand off the work without you. They won't "loop you in" as an afterthought. They'll come to you first—because *you're* the reason they came to the firm at all.

*That's the whole point.*

You're not just memorable. You're untouchable. But if the client starts calling the other partner directly? You're out. And that origination stream you started? Now it's under someone else's name.

## Protect the Relationship Before You Cross-Sell

The solution?

You had better get comfortable with having hard conversations—*real quick*. Before the lunch. Before the pitch. Before the matter shows up.

*Ask yourself if you even need that partner in the room.* Because once they're in—it gets complicated.

If a senior partner wants to join you, you don't just smile and say "sounds great." You ask: *"If something comes out of this, how are we handling origination?"*

*Is it uncomfortable? Hell yeah!*

But not nearly as uncomfortable as pretending it didn't matter—then seeing the matter come through *without* your name on it.

You're a partner now. That means you don't wait to be protected. You set the terms before the door even opens.

*But what if you hate confrontation?*

There are ways to protect yourself without confrontation or drama—but you have to be intentional. The attorneys I work with know exactly how to create clarity, on the record, before credit becomes an issue. If you don't, you'll keep getting written out of relationships you started. And once that happens, it's a lot harder to claw your way back in.

## You Brought the Client. Start Acting Like It.

Getting credit isn't a one-time event. It's a cadence. You don't just bring in the client and expect origination to show up forever—you stay in the relationship.

You check in. You stay copied. You loop yourself into what's happening—even if you're not running the matter.

Because the minute you disappear, so does your leverage. And don't assume anyone else is going to remind the firm—or the client—how the relationship started. That's your job. *You brought them in. Start acting like it.*

And here's one more move that makes a difference:

*Even if you're not staffed on the case, let the client know you're still their person.*

If something goes wrong—billing, communication, anything—you're the one they can call. That one line? It keeps you in the center.

Knowing your client as a person—*not just a matter generator*—is foundational.

Rainmaker: Unleashed

When you've built a real relationship, staying in touch isn't awkward. It's not a "check-in." It's a conversation. You remember their wife, son, and daughter went on that Harry Potter tour in Europe. You congratulate them on that nonprofit board they joined. You send a note when you see something relevant to their world.

That's what keeps the connection warm. That's what makes you unforgettable. And when you stay close like that? They don't reroute around you. They pull you in—because you're part of their team, not just the firm's.

And this is exactly how that client becomes a referral source, too. When the relationship is personal, they don't just think of you for their own matters—they recommend you to others.
Because you didn't treat them like a transaction.
In turn, they don't *either*.
They are invested in your success.

You treated them like a human. And that's what people remember. That's what people trust. It's not about being charming. It's about being consistent. When you show up like that? **You don't just protect your origination—you multiply it.**

## Trust, Then Verify

There are times when the hand-off works. When you know the partner. When you've seen how they operate. When you trust them to handle the work—and to respect the relationship.

In those cases, you don't have to fight for every inch of credit. You still protect it. But you're not chasing it. You've built internal equity. You've built the rapport. And the partner keeps you in the loop because they know you're not going away.

*That's what earned trust looks like.*

But even then—*you stay close to the client*. **Because rainmakers don't disappear. They remain visible. Connected. Relevant.**

It's why I'd always check in—grab lunch, ask how things were going.

One time, a client casually told me he liked the woman on the team but wasn't thrilled with the guy handling the matter. That was it. Just one sentence. But because I stayed close, I heard it. And I fixed it. Quietly. Internally.

That's the kind of access you don't get if you disappear after the hand-off.
The client saw me as their point of contact—and their friend.
That's what doesn't show up on the invoice. And that's the difference.

## When Conflicts Kill the Matter—Or Do They?

*I had a client—Bob—a new partner who landed a huge case. He was thrilled. Until he ran conflicts. The next day, he called me. "It got conflicted out. I lost it." But here's what I told him: Conflicts aren't just yes or no. They come in layers.*

**First***: you're not conflicted—great. Go run the matter.*
**Second***: you're conflicted, but you can still take the case if the firm sets up an ethical wall.*
**Third***: you're fully conflicted, and you really can't touch it.*

*That's when I told him: this is why you build relationships with attorneys outside your firm. When a matter gets blocked, you don't say, "Sorry, good luck." You say, "Let me find someone who can help you."*

**You didn't drop them. You stepped up and solved the problem.**

The client doesn't forget that. You stayed calm, stayed connected, and made their life easier. That's not lost. That's leverage. Now they owe you—for a matter you didn't even touch.

*You pick up the phone, call someone you trust, and say—half-joking, but fully serious—"Quid pro quo." When I'm conflicted, I throw it your way. When you're conflicted, you return the favor.*

*Bob laughed and said, "Of course you'd turn a loss into a win."* Damn right I would.

*The best part:* when you build relationships with counterparts—attorneys outside your firm who do exactly what you do—you don't just save the matter. You create a funnel. A back-and-forth pipeline that benefits both of you.

One conflict turns into two future opportunities. And with the client? You don't disappear. You still check in. You stay close. Now they trust you even more—because you showed them you'd find the right solution, even if it wasn't through you.

*That's not a loss. That's a power play.*

# You Can't Win a Game You Pretend Isn't Happening

Stop looking surprised.
Origination isn't about fairness. It's not about who did the most work. It's about who brought in the client, stayed visible, and made sure everyone knew it.

If you think being excellent is enough, it's not.
If you think the system will reward your effort automatically, it won't.
If you think someone will tap you on the shoulder and explain how to get credit—good luck.

You can't win a game if you don't know the rules. *So learn them. Then flip the board.*

That's why I tell my clients: stop playing nice—and start playing smart.
To stop being grateful and start being strategic.
To stop assuming and start asking.
No one's going to give you origination.
**You claim it. You protect it. And you start now.**

*You've made it to the end—but this isn't the end.* It's the ignition point. You've seen what happens when relationships are built with intention.

When confidence comes from strategy, not swagger. When the system doesn't pick you—**but you rise anyway.**

You know now that rainmaking isn't about scripts, or schmoozing, or chasing. It's about owning your value. Showing up like a force. Playing the long game on your terms.

So stop waiting for someone to tell you you're ready. You are. And everything you need? You just read it. Go build what lasts. And don't ask for permission.

*It's your move now.*

*"I am not afraid. I was born to do this."*

*—Joan of Arc*

# Epilogue: This Was Always About Power

Let's be clear—this *isn't just* about getting clients.
It's about building real power. ***Lasting power.***
Because when you control the revenue, you control your career.
You don't get sidelined. You get a seat.
You don't just stay in the firm. You shape it.

That's the goal.
To get more of you on Management Committees.
In the rooms where decisions get made, compensation gets set, and culture gets defined.

When that table includes *your* voice, *your* strategy, *your* relationships?
You're not just changing your path.
You're shifting what's possible for everyone coming next.

So don't just read this.
Use it.
Protect yourself.
To build what no one can take away.
To step into every room like you belong there—because you do.

**Firm leadership—if retention's a problem and you're serious about fixing it?** Don't just quote this book. Call me.
Implementation is what I do. ***This is my lane.***
You know where to find me.

—Sejal Bhasker Patel
Founder, Sage Ivy Consulting

# About the Author

**Sejal Bhasker Patel** is not your typical consultant—and *Rainmaker: Unleashed* is not your typical book.

A former Big Four strategist, Sejal built **Sage Ivy Consulting** to equip attorneys to turn relationships into revenue—without selling their soul. Her work lives at the intersection of strategy, psychology, and sharp client instincts. She doesn't do fluff. She builds rainmakers.

Sejal partners with law firms ready to invest in their talent—firms that know revenue drives retention, and retention drives revenue. You can't fix one without the other. Through her *Rainmaking Series*, she works directly with high-performing attorneys to build client control, visibility, and power.

Her strategies have been featured in *Above the Law*, delivered inside Am Law 100 firms, and quietly implemented by leaders who know that rainmakers don't just appear—they're developed.

This book is the first step.
**The real power move? Making it firm-wide.**

To bring *Rainmaker: Unleashed* to your firm—through full-scale rainmaking engagement or licensing:
www.sageivyconsulting.com
spatel@sageivyconsulting.com
linkedin.com/in/sbpatel
**Based in NYC — Available nationwide**

Made in the USA
Middletown, DE
06 July 2025